1,2 Chronicles

BIBLE STUDY COMMENTARY

1,2 Chronicles

EUGENE H. MERRILL

Lamplighter
Books Grand Rapids,
Michigan
Zondervan Publishing House

BIBLE STUDY COMMENTARY: 1, 2, CHRONICLES
Copyright © 1988 by Eugene H. Merrill

Lamplighter Books are published by the Zondervan Publishing House
1415 Lake Drive, S.E., Grand Rapids, Michigan 49506

Library of Congress Cataloging-in-Publication Data

Merrill, Eugene H.
1, 2 Chronicles: Bible study commentary / Eugene H. Merrill. p. cm. —
(Bible study commentary series)

"Lamplighter books."
Bibliography: p.
ISBN 0-310-32571-4
1. Bible. O.T. Chronicles—Commentaries. I. Title. II. Title: First, Second
Chronicles. III. Series.
BS1345.3.M47   1988
222'.607—dc19   88–11786
                                                                                    CIP

Edited by John D. Sloan, Nia Jones

Printed in the United States of America

88 89 90 91 92 93 / CH / 10 9 8 7 6 5 4 3 2 1

Contents

Preface

One can imagine few things in life more spiritually rewarding and satisfying than to engage in a concentrated study of the Word of God to clarify its meaning for others. Such has been the case in this endeavor. Particularly enriching has been the opportunity to contribute to a series in which so many esteemed and admired colleagues have had a share.

Unless someone has undertaken such a project, it is difficult to know how indispensable others are to its accomplishment. Although the author pens the words, he achieves his final objectives only because of the dedicated and competent work of his support team. Fairness dictates that they be recognized and thanked.

John D. Sloan, editor of Lamplighter Books, invited the author to write this volume and he and his staff have provided constant and much appreciated guidance along the way. Time for its pursuit was provided by the administration of Dallas Theological Seminary and the author's colleagues at Dallas have offered encouragement and assistance. Most importantly, the seminary made staff and equipment available to accomplish the word processing, printing, and reproduction required.

Special gratitude must go to Mrs. Wendy Mumaw, secretary of the Department of Semitics and Old Testament Studies. Some people view their work grudgingly as a job; others look at it joyfully as a ministry. Wendy, with characteristic self-sacrifice and readiness, went beyond normal expectations to care for

virtually everything between the long-hand originals and the
printed page.

Finally, the author cannot overlook the willingness of his
wife Janet and daughter Sonya Leigh to tolerate his absence
from home and "sacrifice" of the summer of 1987 to this project.
As always, their prayerful understanding and sympathetic
support has made the difference. May the God of Israel whom
Chronicles extols be praised for his goodness and grace in
bringing this happy assignment to its fruition.

Introduction

The Books of 1 and 2 Chronicles provide the only Old Testament example of a "synoptic problem," since they parallel the contents of Samuel and Kings to a great extent. That is, they recount the history and theology of Israel from a slightly different perspective than that of Samuel and Kings. Likewise, the Gospels of Matthew, Mark, and Luke view the life and teachings of Jesus in similar but by no means identical ways. Students of the Old Testament are sometimes confused by this repetitious yet alternative approach to God's revelation. Why, it is asked, should there be two versions of the same set of circumstances and events?

These same kinds of questions have been asked relative to the Gospels. The most satisfying evangelical response has been that each gospel writer was a unique individual who witnessed personally or otherwise came to understand the life and message of Jesus in a unique way. Furthermore, each recounted the tradition as the Spirit of God prompted and corrected him. Thus, the quotations of Jesus' words differ from gospel to gospel and the order of events likewise varies according to the interests, emphases, and literary structures peculiar to each writer. This freedom of literary creativity within the boundaries of divine supervision is well understood and accepted by those who have engaged themselves in serious study of the Gospels.

Careful reading of Samuel-Kings and of Chronicles reveals the same approaches and processes. Though the two respective accounts deal largely with the same essential subject matter, they vary in their emphases, in what they include or exclude, and in their theological interests. And yet, just as reverent gospel studies have shown that there is no demonstrable case for contradiction among them, so Samuel-Kings and Chronicles evidence no insoluble disharmonies. The exposition to follow will make this clear.

To see Chronicles as synoptic to Samuel-Kings is not to deny its independent importance and significance, for it is in those very areas of its topical, thematic, and theological divergences that its justification lies. Its authors and compilers were sensitive to the fact that the Holy Spirit desired to use them to communicate the truth of revelation in ways that paralleled the message of Samuel-Kings from a different perspective and with different objectives. Thus, no study of the Old Testament is complete that dismisses Chronicles as a mere repetition of Samuel-Kings and fails to see it for what it is—a fresh, alternative way to view God's dealings with his people in Old Testament times.

Name

The title "Chronicles" comes from the Latin name for the books proposed by Jerome, *Chronicon totius divinae historiae* ("a chronicle of the whole of sacred history"), a most appropriate way to describe its contents. The Hebrew title is *dibrê hayyāmîm* ("an account of the past," an approximate translation). This very phrase occurs in 1 Chronicles 27:24, clearly referring to a genre of history-writing known technically as "annals." The Greek Old Testament (the Septuagint) assigns the title *Paraleipomenon* to Chronicles ("things omitted"). This suggests that the Books of Chronicles contain information lacking in the parallel accounts of Samuel and Kings.

Authorship and Sources

There is no hint in Chronicles itself, or indeed anywhere else in the Bible, as to who wrote these books. In fact, it may not even be appropriate to think in terms of authorship at all for, as all scholars recognize, Chronicles consists of a collection of a great many documents brought together as in an anthology. The author of Chronicles might be best described as an editor or, as is done throughout this commentary, simply "chronicler." At any rate, this does not affect matters of inspiration and canonicity for the Holy Spirit led throughout the process of authorship and collection of the material to ensure its absolute reliability, a fact that its canonicity itself attests.

The principal written sources cited in 1 and 2 Chronicles are as follows:

1. Book of the Kings of Israel and Judah (2 Chron. 27:7; 35:27; 36:8)
2. Book of the Kings of Judah and Israel (2 Chron. 16:11; 25:26; 28:26; 32:32)
3. Book of the Kings of Israel (1 Chron. 9:1; 2 Chron. 20:34; 33:18)
4. Commentary on the Book of the Kings (2 Chron. 24:27)
5. The History of Samuel, Nathan, and Gad (1 Chron. 29:29)
6. The Prophecy of Ahijah and Visions of Iddo (2 Chron. 9:29)
7. The History of Shemaiah and History of Iddo (2 Chron. 12:15)
8. The Commentary of Iddo (2 Chron. 13:22)
9. The History of the Prophet Jehu and a Writing of Isaiah (2 Chron. 26:22)
10. A History of the Seers (2 Chron. 33:19)
11. The Early Chronicles of David (1 Chron. 27:24)
12. The Laments (2 Chron. 35:25)

The first three of these may appear to be the same as the canonical books of 1 and 2 Kings, but there are some things referred to in these sources of Chronicles that do not appear in the biblical Kings (cf. 1 Chron. 9:1; 2 Chron. 27:7; 33:18; 36:8). It is clear, in any case, that the chronicler had at his disposal a vast noncanonical literature that is no longer extant but that he knew to be reliable as source material.

Date

The last datable event in Chronicles is the decree of Cyrus (2 Chron. 36:22–23) issued in 538 B.C. after the fall of Babylon to the Persians. Clearly, the book in its present form postdates that.

However, the genealogy of David (1 Chron. 3:1–24) lists his royal descendants to Anani, the eighth generation after Jehoiachin (v. 24). Jehoiachin was eighteen years old in 597 B.C., the year of his captivity by the Babylonians (2 Kings 24:8). An average of twenty-five years for a generation would yield a date for Anani about 400 B.C., so one could make a case for the final stage of the Chronicles composition at about that time.

The Talmudic treatise *Baba Bathra* appears to attribute the authorship of Chronicles to Ezra, the famous scribe who returned to Jerusalem in 458 B.C. There is no way to know how long after his return he lived, but it is unlikely that he would have known Anani. Moreover, there is nothing in the *Baba Bathra* statement that says Chronicles was completed by Ezra, but only that he "wrote the genealogy of Chronicles unto himself" (15a). This leaves room for genealogical records beyond his own time and, of course, it may intend to say only that Ezra contributed to the genealogies and to nothing else.

There is some evidence, finally, that the crucial passage in the Davidic genealogy, 1 Chronicles 3:17–24, is not a straight line of descent from Jehoiachin through Anani but that some of the persons named were contemporaneous and not successive (cf. 1 Chron. 3:17–24 below). Even so, there are at least five generations including Anani so that a mid-fifth century date is still most likely. This obviously would permit Ezra to be none other than the chronicler but does not prove it. It seems best to let the chronicler remain an anonymous compiler or editor who flourished in the latter part of the fifth century.

Purpose and Structure

These two elements are so mutually informative it is best to consider them together. After a lengthy and detailed genealogical section (1 Chron. 1–9), designed to trace David and his royal descendants back to the patriarchs and eventually to Adam himself, the historian nearly ignores Saul (whose reign is of great interest to the author of Samuel; cf. 1 Sam. 9–31) in his desire to arrive at his real center of attention—the Davidic Monarchy.

The Saul story occupies only fourteen verses (1 Chron. 10) and appears to have been written in a very negative tone. The rise of David, his flight from Saul, and the seven-and-a-half-year reign at Hebron are all but ignored (1 Chron. 11:1–3). The chronicler in effect begins at Jerusalem and through the remainder of 1 Chronicles (11:4–29:30) relates in glowing terms the military and particularly the spiritual successes of David.

Continuing with his exaltation to the Davidic kingship in 2 Chronicles, the historian deals in detail with Solomon (cf. 1–9) and then the remaining kings of Judah, emphasizing especially the reigns of the godly kings Jehoshaphat (17:1–20:37), Hezekiah (29:1–32:33), and Josiah (34:1–35:27). This emphasis is evident in the fact that ten out of twenty-seven chapters are devoted to these three kings (out of a total of nineteen kings plus Athaliah). Contrary to the account of 1 and 2 Kings, there is barely any mention of the kings of Israel and when they do appear in the narratives they play an incidental and antagonistic role for the most part.

Several conclusions emerge from these brief observations. First, the dominant theme of Chronicles is the rise, success, and descent of King David. The book is monarchy-centered. But the monarchy does not float free of historical and theological moorings, for it was established on the basis of covenant promises that find their roots in the very beginning of the human race and in the patriarchs. It is also a monarchy of universalistic dimensions, for it is not attached covenantally to Moses and the Law but reaches outside and beyond that narrow compass. Chronicles begins with the human race as a whole and closes open-ended, with a view to the ongoing of God's people as a vehicle of redemptive grace for all mankind.

One should also note that the Davidic monarchy appears in an almost exclusively good light. Missing are many of the tawdry and unflattering narratives found in Samuel, such as David's adultery, his murder of Uriah, the rape and murder among his children, and Absalom's rebellion. The chronicler surely knew of these things and was not trying to hide them. His purpose, however, was not served by them, for he was interested in the theological meaning and purpose of the monarchy and not those circumstances that threatened to undo it.

It is also important to observe that matters of cult, temple, and priesthood far outweigh those of politics and warfare all through the chronicler's work. There is much focus on priestly and Levitical genealogies (1 Chron. 6:1–81; 9:1–34), temple planning and construction (1 Chron. 13:1–14; 15:1–17:27; 21:28–26:32; 28:1–29:22; 2 Chron. 2:1–8:16), and the faithful carrying out of religious tradition (esp. 2 Chron. 20:5–13, 24–30; 23:12–21; 24:4–14; 29:2–31:21; 34:2–35:19). Particularly striking is the priestly role assigned to the king, a role that blends the two offices into one (1 Chron. 15:25–28; cf. 2 Sam. 6:12–15; Ps. 2; 110). Thus, David and his descendants provided a type of the royal priesthood that would find culmination and fulfillment in Jesus Christ (cf. Heb. 6:13–8:13).

There could hardly have been a more fitting and encouraging message for the post-exilic Jewish community than that of Chronicles. The people had returned, a temple had been rebuilt, and a cultus with its priesthood and other institutions continued. There was no monarchy, to be sure, but the merging of the offices of priest and king along with the prophetic promises of contemporary men of God, such as Haggai (2:4–9) and Zechariah (9:9–10; 14:9–21), were reason enough to fill the remnant with hope that the covenant promises of the Lord could not fail and would surely come to pass.

Outline

I. The Genealogies (1 Chron. 1:1–9:44)
   A. The Patriarchal Genealogies (1:1–54)
      1. The Genealogy of Adam (1:1–4)
      2. The Genealogy of Japheth (1:5–7)
      3. The Genealogy of Ham (1:8–16)
      4. The Genealogy of Shem (1:17–27)
      5. The Genealogy of Abraham (1:28–34)
      6. The Genealogy of Esau (1:35–54)
   B. The Genealogy of Judah (2:1–4:23)
      1. The Sons of Israel (2:1–2)
      2. The Sons of Judah (2:3–4)
      3. The Sons of Perez and Zerah (2:5–8)
      4. The Genealogy of Hezron (2:9–41)
      5. The Genealogy of Caleb (2:42–55)
      6. The Genealogy of David (3:1–24)

Chapter 1

The Genealogies
(1 Chronicles 1:1–9:44)

Though frequently dismissed as tedious and unimportant by many readers of the Bible, the genealogies in Chronicles have come to be understood as having profound historical and theological importance. Many tribal peoples to this day identify themselves and assert their worth, dignity, and significance to the extent that they can trace their roots to the ancestors for whom they were named and who account for their origins. This was no less true in the ancient Near Eastern nomadic world of which Israel was a part.

The purpose of the genealogies of 1 Chronicles 1:1–9:44 is to trace the lineage of the twelve tribes of Israel from the final days of Old Testament history back through their father Israel or Jacob and through Abraham, Eber, Shem, and Noah to the first man of all, Adam. The post-exilic nation, that is, the Jews who returned from Babylon after 538 B.C., could thus remain confident of its theological and historical connections and of its mission to the world as a chosen people. Without interruption they could establish their link to the father of the elect nation (Jacob) and to the founder of the elect seed (Abraham) who was called out of the world of men but who at the same time was directly a part of them by virtue of common ancestry from Adam. They might have sinned against God and have gone into Babylonian exile, but they were back again in the land and ready to take up their covenant responsibilities and privileges to which their genealogical structures so eloquently testified.

A. The Patriarchal Genealogies (1:1–54)

1. The Genealogy of Adam (1:1–4)

The first section of genealogy, which covers the period from Creation to the Flood, consists of eleven generations from Adam through the three sons of Noah inclusively. It is in effect a summation of the genealogical record of Genesis 5:1–32, and like the Genesis text, it ends with a division of the single line into three branches. Its purpose is to trace the continuity from Adam, with whom God had made the original covenant mandate (Gen. 1:26–28), to Shem, the son of Noah, through whom that mandate would be carried out in the post-diluvian world (Gen. 9:25–27).

2. The Genealogy of Japheth (1:5–7)

Though the name Shem usually appears first in accounts of Noah's sons, it comes last in their respective genealogies here because of climactic and dramatic effect. It is noteworthy that the Japheth line is traced for only two generations through two segmented lines. Of the seven sons listed (the same appear in Gen. 10:2–4), the sons of only two of them, Gomer and Javan, are listed. Gomer most likely is the patronymic for the Cimmerians, native to the region north and east of the Black Sea. Javan is a variation of Ionia, the land of the ancient Greeks on the coast of Asia Minor. The reason for the inclusion of only the descendants of Gomer and Javan lies in the fact that the Cimmerians (contemporary to and replaced by the Scythians) and Greeks had emerged by the time of the composition of Chronicles as two of the major world powers. This, of course, had already been anticipated in Genesis 10.

3. The Genealogy of Ham (1:8–16)

The names of the descendants of Ham here are exactly the same as those of Genesis 10:6–20, but the narrative of Nimrod and other expansions found in Genesis do not appear in Chronicles. Of the four sons of Ham, three gave rise to African peoples, while the fourth, Canaan, occupied the eastern Mediterranean coast, the later Palestine. Scholars universally identify Cush (vv. 8–9) as Nubia or Ethiopia, Mizraim (vv. 11–12) as

Egypt, and Put, whose sons are not listed, as Libya. The affairs of Ethiopia, Egypt, Libya, and of course, Canaan commingled with the affairs of the post-exilic Jewish community and so naturally find a prominent place in the genealogy. Of special interest is the reference to the Philistines (v. 12) who are said to have descended from the Caphtorim, the earliest settlers of Crete. The Philistines, then, found their origins in Ham and came to Canaan via Crete as a part of the Sea Peoples' conquests of Canaan about 1200 B.C. (cf. Deut. 2:23; Jer. 47:4; Amos 9:7).

4. The Genealogy of Shem (1:17–27)

The sons of Shem, nine in number, are the progenitors of the Semitic peoples. Out of the Semites came the Hebrews, the most theologically important element of this people. The chronicler's list in vv. 17–23 parallels Genesis 10:21–29 and 11:10–17. Unique to his genealogical register of Shem is the chronicler's mere listing of names without the usual formulae of kinship, years, and the like in vv. 24–27. The names Shem through Peleg were already included in vv. 17–19, but the names Reu through Abram occur here for the first time in Chronicles. The basis for this part of the list is clearly Genesis 11:18–26, where the genealogy takes form with the "begat formula."

In the very midst of the list of vv. 24–27 are Eber and Peleg, individuals who are prominent in the Genesis 10 genealogy and in 1 Chronicles 1:17–23. Genesis identifies Shem as "the ancestor of all the sons of Eber" (10:21) and points out that it was in the days of Eber that the earth was divided (10:25), an event that caused him to name his son Peleg (Heb. peleg, "division"). This division most likely refers to the dispersion of mankind following the abandonment of the Tower of Babel, since the Peleg generation comes last in the Genesis 10 genealogy following which is the Babel narrative.

More important, however, is the reference to Eber, a name that undoubtedly is the source of the word "Hebrew" (Heb. ʿibrî). The Hebrews, then, descended from Shem through their patronymic Eber, though Abram himself is the first individual known as a Hebrew according to the biblical record (cf. Gen. 14:13).

5. The Genealogy of Abraham (1:28–34)

The descendants of Abraham are traced through his sons by Hagar (vv. 28–31), Keturah (vv. 32–33), and Sarah (v. 34). Hagar is not named, but since she was the mother of Ishmael (cf. Gen. 16:15) who is mentioned, she is clearly implied. Genesis 25:12–18 locates these twelve sons of Ishmael in the wilderness of Shur, just east of the Nile delta and the Red Sea. The name Tema (v. 30), a desert city 250 miles southeast of Petra, suggests that they spread far to the east and so must have occupied the whole Negev, upper Sinai, and trans-Arabah desert areas. Scholars unanimously identify them as Arab tribes.

The sons of Keturah (vv. 32–33), first appearing in Genesis 25:1–4, are six in number, Jokshan and Midian being most important. The identity of the former is not clear but Midian is the father of the Midianites, nomadic folk who ranged throughout the Syro-Arabian wilderness and who played a most important role throughout Israel's history (cf. Exod. 2:18; Num. 22; 25; 31; Judg. 6; etc.). With the offspring of Ishmael they are regarded as progenitors of the Arabs; in fact, the names Ishmaelite and Midianite are often used interchangeably (cf. Gen. 37:28).

The descent of Abraham's family through Sarah (who, like Hagar, is unmentioned) receives only summary treatment here (v. 34), since both sons of Isaac, Esau and Israel (or Jacob), get detailed treatment in the ensuing genealogies.

6. The Genealogy of Esau (1:35–54)

Esau's progeny occur in two sections—his sons and their children (vv. 35–37) and the Edomite kings who preceded the days of Israel's monarchy (vv. 43–54). Between the two parts is the genealogy of Seir, the patronymic of the Seirites who were the pre-Edomite inhabitants of the region to the east and south of the Dead Sea (vv. 38–42; cf. Gen. 36:20–30). The connection between the clans of Esau and Seir is the marriage of Timna, sister of Lotan (v. 39; cf. Gen. 36:22), son of Seir, to Eliphaz, son of Esau (cf. Gen. 36:12). Thus, the indigenous Horites (cf. Gen. 36:20) themselves affiliated with Esau and together developed the nation of Edom (Gen. 36:8; cf. 32:3).

The eight kings of Edom listed in vv. 43–50 appear, with slight spelling variations, in Genesis 36:31–39. Their identities are otherwise unknown, and no apparent link can be made between them and the Esau genealogy of vv. 35–42. Likewise, the eleven "chiefs" (Heb. *'allūpîm)* of verses 51–54 are attested in Genesis 36:40–43. The difference between the "king" and the "chief" here is not clear though the Hebrew *' allūp* elsewhere communicates a military meaning (Exod. 15:15; Zech. 9:7). What is apparent is that the Edomite kings were not dynastic and that successive kings ruled not from a central capital but from their own cities.

The purpose of the rather extensive Esau genealogy lies in the close, brotherly relationship between Esau and Jacob. But the list appears also because of Edom's chronically hostile association with Israel throughout their common history. Edom, in fact, came to typify fraternal disloyalty and the very essence of anti-God rebellion (Obad.; Isa. 34; 63:1–6; Jer. 49:7–22).

B. The Genealogy of Judah (2:1–4:23)

Because one of the major purposes of Chronicles is to extol the dynasty of David, it is fitting that the historian should establish the tribal affiliation of David and commence his account of tribal genealogies with that of Judah. He begins with the descent of Judah that leads directly to David through Hezron (2:3–17), continues with other descendants of Hezron (2:18–55), traces the line of David to his own time (ca. 400 B.C.) (3:1–24), and then either repeats certain genealogical information or adds new detail concerning the Judahites (4:1–23).

1. The Sons of Israel (2:1–2)

The purpose of this list is to connect the following tribal genealogies with the patriarchal genealogies that have already appeared. Israel was the son of Isaac and grandson of Abraham (1:34) so he provides the link to Judah, the tribe of David.

2. The Sons of Judah (2:3–4)

Shortly after Jacob had returned to Canaan from Haran, his son Judah married a Canaanite by whom he had three sons: Er, Onan, and Shelah (Gen. 38:1–5). The first of these died for unspecified reasons and Onan, who failed to honor his brother by siring children in his name, died as well (Gen. 38:6–10). Judah then took his own daughter-in-law Tamar and deceitfully fathered twin sons by her (Gen. 38:18, 27–30), Perez and Zerah by name. In this manner the ancestry of David came about.

3. The Sons of Perez and Zerah (2:5–8)

Of the two sons of Perez, only Hezron is important here for he appears in David's ancestral line (v. 9). The sons of Zerah are included primarily because of their appearance in the story of Achar (Achan in Josh. 7:1) who sinned by taking for himself items that were devoted to the Lord in the destruction of Jericho under Joshua (Josh. 7:16–26). As that account makes clear, Achar was the son of Carmi, the son of Zabdi (Zimri in 1 Chron. 2:6), the son of Zerah. In both Chronicles and Joshua, however, "son" must not be pressed too literally for in 1 Kings 4:31, Ethan, Heman, Calcol, and Darda (Dara in most manuscripts of 1 Chron. 2:6) are called sons of Mahol and not of Zerah. It is also in the chronicler's interest to include these same names because Ethan and Heman served as temple musicians under David (1 Chron. 15:16–19) and they, as well as Calcol and Darda, were poets and sages to whom Solomon was favorably compared (1 Kings 4:29–31).

4. The Genealogy of Hezron (2:9–41)

The line of Hezron results in the family of David through Hezron's son Ram. The list here (vv. 9–15) is the same as that of Ruth 4:18–22 and Matthew 1:3–6 except for the chronicler's addition of the brothers of Ram (Jerahmeel and Caleb, v. 9) and the brothers and sisters of David (vv. 13–16) as well as his nephews Abishai, Joab, Asahel, and Amasa (vv. 16–17).

Jerahmeel and Caleb themselves produced noteworthy offspring and their genealogies follow in reverse order. There is first an abbreviated list for Caleb (2:18–20) with a longer one following (2:42–55). By his three wives he had four sons, the last of whom, Hur, was father to Uri and grandfather to Bezalel. This same Bezalel was one of the overseers for the construction of the wilderness tabernacle (Exod. 31:2; 35:30; 38:22; 2 Chron. 1:5) so obviously he was not the sixth generation of an unbroken succession from Judah. That would suggest only six generations in a period of four-hundred-and-fifty years (ca. 1900–1450 B.C.) from the birth of Perez to the erection of the tabernacle.

Before the historian continues to discuss the descent of Jerahmeel, he relates a narrative concerning another wife of Hezron, the daughter of Makir (2:21–24). Makir elsewhere is the son of Manasseh (Gen. 50:23; Num. 26:29) and the father of Gilead (Josh. 17:1–3). This means that Gilead was the great-grandson of Joseph, a fact that suits Hezron's age (sixty, v. 21) when he married Makir's daughter. Segub, the son of this union, was the father of Jair "who controlled twenty-three towns in Gilead" (2:22). These towns (or Havvoth Jair if Heb. ḥavvōt is a place name here), along with the town of Kenath and its surrounding settlements, fell to Geshur and Aram. Aram (not to be confused with Aramea) cannot be identified but Geshur was a tiny state east of Mount Hermon. Havvoth Jair was originally identical to Argob or Bashan, the Amorite kingdom adjacent to Geshur and Maacah (Deut. 3:13–14). Kenath was a town in or near Argob that fell to a certain Nobah in the days of the Israelite conquest. It then took the name Nobah (Num. 32:42; Judg. 8:11).

The descent, then, is Hezron-Segub-Jair. Since, however, Jair is none other than the judge of Israel by that name (Judg. 10:3–5), there clearly are names missing in the genealogical linkage between Hezron and Jair. The purpose of this brief narrative (vv. 21–23) is to show that the Gileadites were related to Israel by virtue of Hezron's marriage into the family of Makir, the father of Gilead (vv. 21, 23b). A final offspring of Hezron is Ashhur, father of Tekoa (2:24), whose brief genealogy appears later (4:5–7). From Ashhur sprang the little kingdom of the Ashurites on the Jezreel plain (2 Sam. 2:9).

The chronicler next addresses the genealogy of Jerahmeel (2:25–41), the third son of Hezron (2:9). His descendants, whose names appear only here, produced the Jerahmeelite tribe of seminomads who ranged throughout the Negev in the days of David (1 Sam. 27:10; 30:29). Of some interest is the marriage of the daughter of Sheshan (no doubt the Ahlai of 2:31) to an Egyptian servant Jarha (2:34–35). This may place Sheshan as early as the period of the Israelite sojourn in Egypt.

5. The Genealogy of Caleb (2:42–55)

Once again the focus is on the descendants of Caleb; this time, in a more complete delineation (2:42–55; cf. 2:18–20). The first section (vv. 42–49) appears to deal with sons of Caleb by wives other than those listed before (vv. 18–19). Notable among them are Ziph (v. 42), whose tribe, the Ziphites, provided residence for David in his days of flight from Saul (1 Sam. 23:14–15). Hebron, son of Mareshah and grandson of Caleb, gave his name to the famous city of Hebron, where David first reigned over Judah (2:42; cf. 2 Sam. 2:1–4). Since the city bore this name at least as early as the time of Moses (Gen. 13:18; 23:2, 19; 35:27; Num. 13:22), it is evident that this Caleb must not be confused with Caleb the friend of Joshua, who received Hebron as his inheritance in Canaan (Josh. 14:13–14). But the Caleb of verse 49 must also refer to the earlier person because there is no other reference here to the later Caleb. The intent of the historian is to identify Acsah, otherwise known as the daughter of the later Caleb (Judg. 1:12), as the daughter (i.e., descendant) of the earlier Caleb as well.

Still another Caleb (and his genealogy) occurs in the Hezron line (2:50–55). This one is the son of Hur by his wife Ephrathah (or Ephrath, 2:19), thus grandson of the earlier Caleb (2:19). Among his descendants were Shobal, father (founder?) of Kiriath-Jearim, and Salma, father (founder?) of Bethlehem, two towns of special interest to David, the latter particularly as his birthplace. The chronicler also points out that the scribal clans of Jabez, who were Kenites by location, likewise descended from Salma (2:55). A prominent scion of that line was Recab, who gave rise to a devout and observant clan in later Israelite history (Jer. 35:1–19).

6. The Genealogy of David (3:1–24)

This is the centerpiece of the chronicler's lengthy treatment of genealogies as well as the climax of the tracing of the Judahite line. The first part (vv. 1–9) lists the six sons of David born in the years at Hebron and the nine born subsequently at Jerusalem. Especially prominent, of course, is Solomon, son of

Bathsheba (3:5), because it was he through whom the dynastic succession passed (1 Kings 1:13, 17, 30).

The remainder of the genealogy consists of a list of the royal Davidic line to the end of the kingdom of Judah (586 B.C.) and even beyond. The names prior to the Exile agree with those of the kings and princes that otherwise appear in the historical records of Kings and Chronicles except for Johanan, the eldest son of Josiah (3:15), who is otherwise unknown. Shallum, the fourth son (3:15), must be the same as Jehoahaz who was the first of Josiah's sons to succeed him on the throne (2 Kings 23:30–31; cf. Jer. 22:11). It is clear that he was not the eldest son, however, for he was younger even than Jehoiakim (2 Kings 23:36; cf. 23:31).

The descent following the deportation begins with the sons of Jehoiachin, Shealtiel and Pedaiah, the latter being the father of Zerubbabel (3:17–19). The difficulty here is that Zerubbabel elsewhere is called the son of Shealtiel (Ezra 3:2, 8; 5:2; Neh. 12:1; Hag. 1:12, 14; 2:2, 23; Matt. 1:12; Luke 3:27). With such overwhelming evidence against Pedaiah as father of Zerubbabel, one may conclude either that Pedaiah died and Zerubbabel was adopted by Shealtiel or that Pedaiah was in fact not Shealtiel's brother but his son so that Zerubbabel was the grandson of Shealtiel. The latter has in its favor a completion of what otherwise appears to be a meaningless isolation of the name as "Shealtiel his son" (v. 17).

Further complication attends the list as recorded by Luke who identifies Shealtiel as the son of Neri (Luke 3:27), a descendant of David through his son Nathan, not Solomon (3:31). This accords well with the statement that Jehoiachin left no male heir (Jer. 22:30) and yet had "sons" (1 Chron. 3:17). These sons could have been offspring of a daughter of Jehoiachin who married Neri, the descendant of David in a parallel line. Shealtiel, Pedaiah, Zerubbabel, and the others would thus be heirs of David through Solomon and offspring of Jehoiachin by marriage, and Neri, Shealtiel, and Zerubbabel would be David's descendants through his son Nathan. The chronicler lists the descendants of Zerubbabel through his son Hananiah (3:19); Luke does so through another son Rhesa (Luke 3:27). Matthew knew of still another tradition and identifies Abiud as the son of Zerubbabel through whom the messianic line came down to Jesus himself (Matt. 1:13). Abiud does not appear in the chronicler's list but there is no reason to think that the lists that have survived are at all complete. Shemaiah, in fact, is credited with six sons but only five are named (1 Chron. 3:22) so Zerubbabel may have had sons named Abiud (Matt. 1:13) and Rhesa (Luke 3:27), neither of whom is attested in an Old Testament genealogy.

The chronicler obviously does not trace the genealogies past his own time so the further descendants of David through Zerubbabel (and perhaps otherwise) continue for only two or three more generations (3:21–24). Hananiah, a son of Zerubbabel, has only one generation in his succession. Then there follow four families whose connection is unstated, with the last of these extending through five generations—Shecaniah, Shemaiah, Neariah, Elioenai, and Anani. If Shecaniah was contemporary with Hananiah, the son of Zerubbabel (which seems reasonable), five generations inclusive would place the date of Anani, the last named, about 425 B.C., a generally accepted date for Chronicles.

7. The Genealogy of Judah (4:1–23)

Having dealt with the genealogy of Judah to establish the Judahite connections of David and his dynasty, the chronicler now views it from a broader context and in more narrative terms. Some of the same names occur but others appear for the first time and for reasons that are not altogether obvious to the modern reader.

The record begins with reference to Perez, son of Judah, and various other descendants (4:1). Hezron is son of Perez; Carmi is son of Zerah, brother of Perez (2:5–6); Hur is grandson of Hezron (2:18–19); and Shobal the grandson of Hur (2:50). Hur's descendants were the Zorathites (4:2) and the Bethlehemites (4:3–4; cf. 2:50–54); hence, the chronicler's interest in the Hur genealogy.

Descendants of Ashhur, previously identified as a posthumous son of Hezron (2:24), form various otherwise unidentifiable clans (4:5–7). Jabez, perhaps to be associated with that place name (2:55), stands out as a man of faith who successfully claimed God's blessing for a large inheritance (4:9–10).

The "men of Recah" (vv. 11-12) remain unknown, but the "sons of Kenaz" (vv. 13–14), the brother of Caleb (Josh. 15:17), are Othniel (also Caleb's son-in-law, Judg. 1:13) and Seraiah. Othniel was Israel's first judge (Judg. 3:9) and Seraiah's son Joab established a center of craftsmanship. Caleb himself had a grandson named Kenaz (4:15). The "sons of Jehallelel" (4:16) can no longer be identified nor can "the sons of Ezrah" (4:17). However, the wife of Mered, one of Ezrah's sons, was ancestress of the Eshtemoaites in addition to being a daughter of Pharaoh (4:18)! This reference is so enigmatic and devoid of solid context, however, that one can hardly assign it a chronological date. Nor is the reference to Mered's Judaean wife (4:18) useful historically for the names involved cannot be otherwise established. A similar verdict applies to all the names of vv. 19–20.

The last section of the Judah genealogy (4:21–23) deals, interestingly enough, with Shelah, the only surviving son of Judah by his Canaanite wife (Gen. 38:5). Of special note is the fact that Shelah named his son Er after his brother whom the Lord had slain (Gen. 38:7). Others of his descendants involved themselves in the linen industry (4:21), in rule over Moab (4:22), and in royal pottery manufacture at Gederah, in the shephelah of Judah (Josh. 15:36). The records concerning all this, the chronicler adds, are from "ancient times" (4:22).

C. The Genealogy of Simeon (4:24–43)

Judah, the fourth son of Jacob, appears first in the chronicler's genealogy because of David's Judean ancestry. The position of Simeon, the second son, right after Judah is because of Simeon's lack of separate tribal allotment (Josh. 19:1) and its eventual loss of identity by assimilation into Judah (cf. 1 Chron. 4:27). The names of the sons of Simeon in verse 24 differ somewhat in spelling from the list in Genesis 46:10 (which adds the name Ohad), but the chronicler's rendition agrees almost perfectly with that of Numbers 26:12–13.

The remainder of the Simeon genealogy has no parallels but some important historical data emerge that shed light on Israel's history. Up to the time of David, the historian says, Beersheba,

Hormah (Tel Masos, five miles southeast of Beersheba), and Ziklag (fifteen miles northwest of Beersheba) were the principal sites of Simeonite habitation (4:31). Later, perhaps in the days of Hezekiah (4:41), settlement centered at Gedor, a place of good pasturage (vv. 39–40). If this is the same as Gerar (thus the Septuagint), the reference to the region as a former Hamite location becomes clear for Gerar was on the border of Egypt, the home of the Hamites. The residue of the Hamites as well as Meunites came under attack by certain Simeonites who put them to death (4:41). The identity of Meun or the Meunites is unclear though they do appear again with reference to Uzziah's campaigns in the Negev (2 Chron. 26:7).

The narrator finally points out that 500 Simeonites went to Seir (i.e., Edom) and slew the Amalekites who had escaped, presumably from the encounter at Gedor just described (4:42–43). This suggests that the Amalekites, who lived in the vicinity of the Egyptian border (1 Sam. 15:4–8), were either identical to the Hamites (or Meunites) or made up a third element at Gedor. Their removal from the hill country of Seir allowed the Simeonites to live there until at least the time the Book of Chronicles was written (v. 43).

D. The Genealogy of Reuben (5:1–10)

Reuben comes next for consideration either because he was Jacob's eldest son (v. 1) or (and more likely) because of the geographical proximity of Reuben's inheritance to that of Judah and Simeon. In fact, the record states that Reuben appears after Judah precisely because Reuben, by his incestuous relationship with his father's concubine (Gen. 35:22), had thereby lost the rights of the firstborn. The result was that Judah became the "royal" tribe through whom the ruler came (cf. Gen. 49:8–12), while Joseph (i.e., Ephraim, Joseph's son) succeeded his father as the principal heir (Gen. 48:8–22; cf. Gen. 49:22–26). Reuben is thus relegated to a lower position.

Reuben's genealogy is not complete. It lists his four sons (v. 3; cf. Num 26:5–11, where several more generations appear) and then selected individuals who distinguished themselves one way or the other. Beerah, a descendant of Reuben through Joel, was among the captives taken to Assyria by Tiglath-Pileser

(745-727 B.C.) in one of his campaigns (vv. 4–6; cf. 2 Kings 15:29). Other clans related to Joel settled from Aroer (on the Arnon River) in the South to Nebo and Baal Meon (on the south border of Gilead) eastward all the way to the Syro-Arabian desert that extended to the Euphrates River (vv. 7–9). These Reubenites waged war with the Hagrites in the time of Saul, a campaign more fully spelled out in vv. 18–22.

E. The Genealogy of Gad (5:11–17)

Gad follows Reuben because of geographical proximity of settlement. They lived in Bashan, occupying a territory extending from that of Reuben in the South to Salecah, a city of the Amorite King Og (Deut. 3:10), far to the east of the Sea of Galilee (v. 11). It is clear that Gilead must have been synonymous with or a part of Bashan, a point made in this passage itself (v. 16).

Various descendants of Gad, whose relationship cannot be determined precisely, appear in vv. 12–15. The genealogical records available to the chronicler originated, as he says, in the days of Jotham of Judah (750–735 B.C.) and Jeroboam II of Israel (793–753 B.C.), some three hundred years before his own time (v. 17).

F. The Hagrite Campaign (5:18–22)

The settlement of Gad in Bashan called to mind a significant military operation undertaken by Reuben, Gad, and the half-tribe Manasseh against the Hagrites and their allies (5:18–19), a campaign already cited in connection with the Reuben genealogy (v. 10). This had taken place in the days of Saul, probably as part of his thrust against the Ammonites who had put the city of Jabesh Gilead under siege (1 Sam. 11:1–11). The overwhelming victory with all its spoil and prisoners was possible because God was with his people and this was his battle (vv. 20–22). From that time until the Captivity (probably that of Tiglath-Pileser III of Assyria in 734; cf. 5:6, 26), the offspring of Reuben, Gad, and Manasseh lived in the north Bashan area of the Hagrites.

G. The Genealogy of the Half-Tribe of Manasseh (5:23–26)

The people of this tribe, celebrated for their heroic military exploits (v. 24), settled in the northern part of Bashan as far north as Baal Hermon, known otherwise as Senir (Deut. 3:9) or Mount Hermon (v. 23). Unfortunately they embraced the idolatry of the peoples they had supplanted so they suffered deportation, along with the Gadites and Reubenites (vv. 5, 22), at the hands of Tiglath-Pileser (also known as Pul or Pulu) in 734 B.C.(v. 26; cf. 2 Kings 15:29). They ended up as refugees in the Habor (now Khabur) River Valley, a tributary of the Euphrates, in the towns of Halah, Habor, and Hara (none of which can now be identified) as well as Gozan (Tell Halaf, on the Habor). As late as the chronicler's own time (ca. 450 B.C.), they remained there, evidently not having participated in the return from Exile (v. 26).

H. The Genealogy of Levi (6:1–81)

1. The Line of the Priests (6:1–15)

The first section (6:1–15), which begins with segmented genealogies (1–3), traces thereafter the line of high priests from Eleazar to Jehozadak, the priest who went into Babylonian Exile. Gershon (or Gershom as in v. 16 and several other places in Chronicles), Kohath, and Merari were sons of Levi who became heads of the three Levitical divisions (see below). The priestly transmission was through Kohath alone. Of his four sons, Amram was priest, and of his two sons Aaron and Moses, Aaron alone served as such. Finally, all four sons of Aaron were set apart for priestly service (Exod. 28:1), but only Eleazar filled the office of high priest, at least until the time of David and Solomon. Nadab and Abihu had died because of an indiscretion in sacrifice (Lev. 10:1–2), and for reasons not altogether clear Ithamar was rejected in favor of Eleazar. It does seem likely, however, that Eli (and his descendant Abiathar) was a priest in the line of Ithamar for otherwise the replacement of that line by Zadok of the Eleazar priesthood is difficult to understand (1 Kings 2:27, 35; cf. 1 Sam. 2:27–36). There could be only one line of high priests at a time, but that line might be alternatively that of Eleazar or that of Ithamar. The chronicler suggests, by including only the descent from Eleazar, that that was the only legitimate line.

Ezra's list of priests (Ezra 7:1–5) begins with himself, whom he identifies as a son of Seraiah (v. 1; cf. 1 Chron. 6:14). Ezra cannot be dated earlier than 500 B.C. so Seraiah, who was priest before the Captivity of 586 cannot be his actual father but rather must be two or three generations removed. This suggests that there are names missing in the lists from time to time. A case in point in comparing Ezra's record further is that he eliminates six names found in 1 Chronicles 6:7–10.

2. Non-Priestly Levites (6:16–30)

The second section of the genealogy lists other, non-high priestly, descendants of Levi. Those of his son Gershon (or Gershom) appear first (vv. 17, 20–21; cf. Exod. 6:17; Num. 3:18). Next follow Kohath's offspring (vv. 18, 22–28) and those of Merari (vv. 19, 29–30). The name Amminadab, son of Kohath in verse 22, is a variation for Izhar who otherwise appears as the father of Korah (Exod. 6:21; Num. 16:1; 1 Chron. 6:37–38).

Of greater interest is the identification of Samuel as a descendant of Kohath and thus a Levite (vv. 27–28). Since he descended through Izhar (v. 22) and not Amram, he was not qualified to be a priest. His cultic activities were, therefore, appropriate but stopped short of anything requiring priestly lineage (1 Sam. 1:21; 2:11; 9:11–14; etc.).

3. The Levitical Musicians (6:31–48)

The third section of the genealogy pertains to the Levites who functioned as temple musicians. These are organized around Heman (v. 33), who is identified as the grandson of Samuel and descendant of Kohath (vv. 33–38); Asaph, descendant of Gershom (vv. 39–43); and Ethan of the line of Merari (vv. 44–47). Heman (not the same as the Heman of 1 Chron. 2:6) appears in narrative passages as a temple singer (1 Chron. 15:17, 19; 16:41–42; 2 Chron. 5:12) and in the title of Psalm 88. Asaph serves along with Heman in the passages just cited and appears to have composed or otherwise to have been associated with several psalms (50, 73, 74, 75, 76, 77, 78, 79, 80, 81, 82, 83).

Ethan is mentioned only two other times (1 Chron. 15:17, 19), both along with Heman and Asaph.

4. The Ministry of the Priests (6:49–53)

The next part of the genealogy defines more precisely the work of the priests, primarily of sacrifice and atonement, as opposed to that of the Levites (v. 49; cf. v. 48). Then, in order once more to establish the authority of the Zadokite priesthood, the chronicler traces the line of priests from Aaron to Zadok. The reference to Ahimaaz (v. 53) clarifies that the Zadok in mind is the individual who supplanted Abiathar (1 Kings 2:35; cf. 2 Sam. 15:27) and not the Zadok who was father of Shallum (1 Chron. 6:12).

5. The Settlement of the Levites (6:54–81)

The final element of the Levite genealogy pertains to their settlement assignments. The arrangement here is according to the three major Levitical divisions—the Kohathites (vv. 54–61, 66–70), the Gershomites (vv. 62, 71–76), and the Merarites (vv. 63, 77–81). Because the priests were all Kohathites, their cities all lay within Kohathite territory, an area limited to Judah and Benjamin (vv. 54–60). These included Hebron, Libnah, Beth Shemesh, Geba, and Anathoth, the home of Jeremiah (Jer. 1:1). Non-priestly Kohathites lived in Manasseh (v. 61) and Ephraim's principal towns, Shechem, Gezer, and Aner (vv. 67–70).

The Gershomites settled in both East and West Manasseh, Issachar, Asher, and Naphtali (v. 62), their major cities being Golan, Kedesh of Issachar, and Kedesh Naphtali (vv. 71–76). The Merarites occupied Reuben, Gad, and Zebulun (v. 63), especially the towns of Bezer, Ramoth Gilead, Heshbon, and Jazer (vv. 78–81). Comparison of the total lists here with that of Joshua 21:9–42 reveals that the chronicler includes only forty-two of the forty-eight that Joshua designated and that some of the names are different. This can be easily explained because the chronicler lists the settlement patterns as they existed in his own day, more than nine hundred years after Joshua. Names could (and must) have changed in some cases, and it is possible that some of the towns assigned had never successfully been occupied.

I. The Genealogy of Issachar (7:1–5)

This obviously partial list embraces five named generations including Issachar. The historian observes that this tribe, notorious for its valorous military activity, had 22,600 soldiers who were descendants of Tola alone by the time of David (v. 2). Those deriving from Uzzi totaled 36,000 (v. 4), while the grand sum was 87,000. Since Uzzi was a son of Tola, and his fighting men outnumber those of Tola, the figures for Uzzi must represent a period much later than David. Perhaps the grand total of all descendants of Issachar also comes from that later time (v. 5).

J. The Genealogy of Benjamin (7:6–12)

This abbreviated list conforms to the pattern of others in which no special note is taken, but the Benjamite genealogy appears twice later (8:1–40; 9:35–44) when the objective is to trace the ancestry of Saul. For now the chronicler mentions three sons of Benjamin—Bela, Beker, and Jediael (v. 6). The list of Numbers 26:38–41 names five sons, but only Bela is in common with 1 Chronicles 7:6. Since Benjamin had ten sons (or grandsons) in all, including Bela and Beker (Gen. 46:21), it is possible that Jediael appears by this name only in Chronicles. Moreover, Ahiram of Numbers 26:38 is probably the same as Aharah of 1 Chronicles 8:1 and Beker of 1 Chronicles 7:6, leaving Ashbel of both Numbers 26:38 and 1 Chronicles 8:1 to be none other than Jediael of 1 Chronicles 7:6.

The Benjamite genealogy continues with the sons of Bela (v. 7), none of whose names agrees with those of other lists (Num. 26:40; 1 Chron. 8:4–5). What is clear is that "sons" frequently means descendants so that the five sons of Bela of this genealogy likely are several generations removed from Bela himself. The sons of Beker (v. 8) appear as "the Hushites the descendants of Aher" (i.e. Aharah; v. 12) while the son of Jediael, Bilhan (v. 10), reemerges in the line of his grandson Ehud (v. 10; cf. 8:6). The total number of fighting men of Benjamin was 59,434 (vv. 7, 9, 11), a figure that must have pertained to the time of David since the census of Issachar, which immediately precedes, makes that point (7:2).

K. The Genealogy of Naphtali (7:13)

The names of Naphtali's sons are all that survive in this brief register and except for some variation in spelling, they agree with those of Genesis 46:24 and Numbers 26:48–49.

L. The Genealogy of Manasseh (7:14–19)

The chronicler here establishes a connection between the tribe of Manasseh and the Judahite clan of Hezron by pointing out that Asriel, son of Manasseh, had a brother Makir whose daughter married Hezron (7:14; cf. 2:21). Of Makir Gilead was born. Makir, whose sister's name was Maacah (7:15), also took a wife named Maacah from the Huppites and Shuppites (vv. 15–16). These clans are likely the same as the descendants of Ir (v. 12), one of the sons of Bela of Benjamin (v. 7). Thus the descendants of Judah, Manasseh, and Benjamin are interwoven in the passing of time.

Another famous offspring of Manasseh was Zelophehad, son of Hepher, son of Gilead (Num. 26:32–33), whose failure to have sons prompted Moses to make provisions for the inheritance rights of daughters in such a case (Num. 36:1–9).

Makir is credited with a brief genealogy (vv. 16–17) as is his sister Hammoleketh (v. 18) and Shemida (v. 19), son of Gilead (Num. 26:32), whose descendants, unlike most of the Gileadites, settled in West Manasseh (Josh. 17:2). If Abiezer, the ancestor of Gideon (Judg. 6:11), is the same as the son of Hammoleketh, then this element of Manasseh also settled in the West.

M. The Genealogy of Ephraim (7:20–29)

The fact that this genealogy ends with Joshua, Moses' young colleague (7:27), indicates that the interesting narrative in this passage takes its setting in the period of Israel's sojourn in Egypt. The sons of Ephraim who appear here are peers in light of the clearer statement of succession in Numbers 26:35–37. Thus, Shuthelah, the first son, is the uncle of the second Shuthelah, son of Zabad. The narrative in question describes a raid by native-born men of Gath (a reference perhaps to the early Philistines of preconquest times) upon two of Ephraim's descendants, Ezer and Elead, during which the two were slain (vv. 21–22). Since Ephraim was born in Egypt (Gen. 41:50–52) and spent his life there, Ezer and Elead either had dealings in Canaan during the sojourn era or they were distant, postconquest descendants. The former seems more likely in view of Ephraim's mourning, an obviously personal thing. Moreover, as a result of this loss, Ephraim took another wife and by her produced the line that eventuated in Joshua, at least ten generations later (vv. 23–27).

The genealogy closes with a succinct description of Ephraim's territory (vv. 28–29). It consisted of all the land from the coastal plain east to the Jordan and between a line from Gezer, Bethel, and Naaran on the South and the Jezreel plain on the North. This included also the lands of Manasseh, Ephraim's brother's tribe, as reference to "descendants of Joseph" (v. 29) makes evident.

N. The Genealogy of Asher (7:30–40)

The descent of Asher in verses 30–31 finds exact parallel in Genesis 46:17, but the Numbers 26:44–47 account lacks the name Ishvah. Otherwise the list appears only here. Of interest is the number of military men, 26,000, a fact that again ties the genealogy into the period of David (cf. 7:2).

O. The Genealogy of Benjamin (8:1–40)

1. The General Genealogy (8:1–28)

This repetition of the Benjamin genealogy (cf. 7:6–12) is greatly expanded and provides the ancestral foundation for the kingship of Saul. It begins with five sons of Benjamin rather than three as in the shorter account and calls them Beker Aharah and Jediael Ashbiel (cf. discussion of 7:6–12). Moreover, several of the sons of Bela (vv. 3–4) appear in Genesis 46:21 as Benjamin's sons, actually meaning grandsons. The descent of Jediael (or Ashbel) is traced through his grandson Ehud (v. 6; cf. 7:10), whereas Beker's is omitted altogether in this genealogy.

Beyond this, it is impossible to identify or link names with each other or to place the tantalizing narrative tidbits (vv. 6–8,

12, 13) into any known historical context. All that is clear is that the genealogy ends at a time when leading Benjamites were living in Jerusalem (v. 28); that is, at some time after David captured the city in 1004 B.C.

2. The Genealogy of Saul (8:29–40)

The real focus of the genealogy, of course, is its attention to the immediate ancestry of Saul who was a Benjamite. The general genealogy ends, then, in a more specialized nature.

The geographic center of this branch of the Benjamite tribe is Gibeon, the city made famous because of its treaty with Joshua (Josh. 9:3–15). Unfortunately, the connection between Saul's immediate ancestry and the Benjamite genealogy as a whole cannot be determined because there is no linkage between Jeiel (supplied from 9:35), the great-grandfather of Saul, and any earlier generation. Moreover, the present list omits the name of Ner, grandfather of Saul (supplied, however, by 9:36), as a son of Jeiel (v. 30), though he does appear in v. 33. The line thus is Jeiel, Ner, Kish, and Saul.

The descent of Saul includes his sons Jonathan, Malki-Shua, Abinadab (otherwise called Ishvi in 1 Sam. 14:49), and Esh-Baal (otherwise Ish-Bosheth; cf. 1 Sam. 14:49; 2 Sam. 2:8). The remainder of the genealogy traces Saul's lineage through Jonathan, a matter easily explained because of David's friendship with Jonathan. Merib-Baal (v. 34) is identical to Mephibosheth (2 Sam. 4:4), but the names beyond that are unattested elsewhere in the Bible with the exception of the duplicate list in 1 Chronicles 9:40–44.

P. The Settlers of Jerusalem (9:1–34)

This chapter begins with a summary of all the preceding genealogies (v. 1a) and an introduction to the lists of Judaeans who had returned from Babylonian Exile (v. 1b). The chronicler first mentions the settlement of sites other than Jerusalem (v. 2) and then Jerusalem itself by the general population (vv. 3–9), the priests (vv. 10–13), the Levites (vv. 14–16), and the temple servants (vv. 17–34).

1. The General Population (9:3–9)

The population of Jerusalem consisted primarily, if not exclusively, of people from Judah, Benjamin, Ephraim, and Manasseh. The Judah clans are divided among Judah's son Perez (v. 4), Shelah (the Shilonites, v. 5), and Zerah (v. 6). The apparently parallel record of Nehemiah 11:4–6 lists different names unless Athaiah (Neh.) is the same as Uthai (Chron.) and Maaseiah (Neh.) is identical to Asaiah (Chron.), which seems unlikely. The different population figures (690 in 1 Chron. 9:6 and 468 in Neh. 11:6) would support the view that totally different lists are in use.

The Benjamites are registered in four clans (vv. 7–8), only one of which, Sallu, appears in Nehemiah (11:7) and even then with different names except for Meshullam, the second in both lists. Varying population totals (956 in Chron. and 928 in Neh.) again argues for different lists. Why the data in Chronicles and Nehemiah that seem to be applying to the same circumstances can be so different is impossible to solve. Most likely, the two accounts are not describing the same events or at least not using the same sources.

2. The Priests (9:10–13)

The list of priests is a greatly truncated version of the full genealogy as is clear from the occurrence of only three names between Meraioth and Azariah (v. 11), whereas the earlier list of priests (6:7–13) had at least twelve. Nehemiah's list (11:10–14) agrees exactly with that of 1 Chronicles 9:10–13, except for Nehemiah's addition of other names at the end and some minor spelling variations. The totals differ again, however, with 1,760 priests in Chronicles and a grand total of 1,192 in Nehemiah.

3. The Levites in General (9:14–16)

The seven families of the Levites, who settled in Jerusalem and "the villages of the Netophathites" (v. 16; i.e. the town of Netophah; cf. Ezra 2:22; Neh. 7:26), appear also in nearly the same form in Nehemiah's account (11:15–18) and with virtually identical spelling of names. This time, however, the chronicler gives no population figures, while Nehemiah says there were "in the holy city" 284 Levites (11:18).

4. The Temple Servants (9:17–34)

In addition to these Levites whose responsibilities must have been related to sacrifice and other more priestly matters were others, such as the gatekeepers. These were divided into four groups with Shallum the Korahite their overall leader. Shallum and his family guarded the King's Gate just to the east of the temple (cf. Ezek. 46:1–2) as had his ancestors Phinehas in the day of the Mosaic tabernacle (Num. 3:32) and Zechariah in the period of the temple of Solomon (v. 21; cf. 1 Chron. 26:2, 14). All the gatekeepers served in a rotating schedule for seven days at a time, coming from the villages that David and Samuel had assigned to their fathers long before them. Since Samuel had died many years before David became king, the reference to Samuel here simply means that David operated according to the inspiration and motivation of the great prophet who had had such a powerful influence over him.

The gatekeepers who served in rotation lived in their villages when not on duty, but the four chief gatekeepers remained at their posts day and night, evidently having living quarters there (vv. 26–27). Altogether there were 212 of them according to the chronicler (v. 22), though Nehemiah gives a total of only 172 (11:19). Nehemiah lists only two groups (those of Akkub and Talmon) so his figure is only a partial account.

Other Levites were responsible for the furnishings and provisions of the house of the Lord (vv. 28–32). This included mixing the spices (cf. Exod. 30:23–25), baking the bread for offerings, and preparing the showbread (cf. Lev. 24:5–9). Still others were singers (v. 33) who, because their work was fulltime, lived in temple apartments. With these the chronicler's listing of the post-exilic population of Jerusalem comes to an end (v. 34).

Q. The Genealogy of Saul (9:35–44)

This account of Saul's genealogy is nearly identical to that of 1 Chronicles 8:29–40, the major differences being the addition of the names Ner (v. 36) and Mikloth (v. 37) here and of the family of Eshek, brother of Azel, in the list of chapter 8 (v. 39). The major point to be made is that the genealogy appears once more because the narrative of Saul's kingship immediately follows (10:1–14). In chapter 8 its purpose was to complete the Benjamite genealogy of which Saul was, of course, a leading member.

For Further Study

1. Read an article on genealogy in a Bible dictionary or encyclopedia. Account for the importance of the genealogies that appear throughout the Bible, especially in Genesis 4, 5, 10, 11; 1 Chron. 1–9; Matthew 1; and Luke 3.

2. Trace Judah and the tribe of Judah through the Bible by means of a concordance. How does the genealogy of Judah in 1 Chronicles 2:1–4:23 contribute to an understanding of Judah's role in the messianic promise?

3. Why was it important that the genealogy of Levi be traced in such detail (1 Chron. 6:1–81)? Read an article on the priesthood in a Bible dictionary or encyclopedia.

4. The census data pertaining to the settlement of Jerusalem after the Babylonian exile was placed at 1 Chronicles 9:1–34, interrupting the normal pattern of genealogy. Why did the chronicler include it here?

Chapter 2

The Rise of David
(1 Chronicles 10:1–22:1)

With the genealogical tables of chapter 1–9 as a background and foundation for the tracing of David's roots through Judah, Israel, Abraham, and eventually Adam, the historian recounts the reign of David through the remainder of 1 Chronicles. By the sheer bulk of material alone (twenty chapters out of sixty-five in 1 and 2 Chronicles), it is clear that the David story is crucial to the chronicler's concern. The writer, therefore, disposes of the reign of Saul in a short genealogy (9:35–44) and a succinct narration of his death (ch. 10) as though to emphasize the illegitimacy of that reign and the desire to get to the real object of his (and God's) attention—the reign of the man after God's own heart.

A. The Death of Saul (10:1–14)

1. The Battle of Gilboa (10:1–6)

The interest of the narrator is focused on the death of Saul and succession of David, so he has little to say about the larger context of the battle between Israel and the Philistines in which these events occurred. (For a full description of that contest, see the commentary on Samuel in this series by Howard F. Vos.) Having administered a sound thrashing to the Israelite troops assembled in the Jezreel Valley and its surrounding heights, the Philistines attacked a pocket of resistance that included Saul and his sons Jonathan, Abinadab, and Malki-Shua (v. 2). The site of this engagement was the mountain of Gilboa, a promontory of 1700 feet that guarded the southerly access from the plain

of Jezreel to the Jordan Valley. When it became apparent to Saul
that he was about to die at the hands of the Philistine bowmen,
he ordered his armor-bearer to slay him for he feared abusive
treatment by the enemy were he to be taken alive. The verb
used here to describe what Saul feared (Heb. *'ālal*) means
essentially to humiliate. What form that humiliation might take
cannot be known but its very thought drove Saul to suicide
(v. 4), one of the few examples of such a death in the Old
Testament (cf. v. 5; 2 Sam. 17:23; 1 Kings 16:18). The reluctance of Saul's attendant to comply with his request no doubt lay
in the same attitude that David had earlier displayed before the
wicked king: "Who can lay a hand on the LORD's anointed and be
guiltless" (1 Sam. 26:9)? Thus, Saul died and, notes the
historian proleptically, so did all his house (i.e., dynasty, v. 6),
preparing the way for the succession of David.

2. The Disposition of Saul (10:7–12)

Meanwhile, Saul's remaining military forces and fellow
citizens who witnessed the debacle at Moriah fled the Jezreel
Valley and abandoned their fields and houses to the victorious
Philistines. The abuse that Saul had feared in life now came
upon him in death for the Philistines found his body, stripped it
of uniform and armor, and decapitated him. This was poetic
justice in a sense for years before their champion Goliath had
suffered a similar fate at the hands of the Israelite David. His
armor had been taken and his head removed as a grisly trophy of
conquest (1 Sam. 17:51, 54).

The armor and head of Saul became symbols of Philistine
superiority as they made their way throughout the cities and
towns of Philistia. One cannot overlook the travels of the ark of
the covenant that the Philistines had captured from Shiloh
nearly a century earlier. That had resulted in ignominious
sickness and shame among the Philistines (1 Sam. 5:1–6:9).
How sweet must this revenge have seemed, even if delayed for
so long a time. Echoes of other early disasters at the hand of
Israel's God also remained vividly in Philistine memory. Those
were the toppling of the idol of their god Dagon before the
presence of the ark (1 Sam. 5:1–5) and the eventual destruction
of the temple of Dagon itself in Samson's final act of vengeance

against his Philistine foes (Judg. 16:28–30). It is not mere coincidence, then, that the Philistines took Saul's armor and his head and displayed them in the temples of their gods (v. 10).

The chronicler omits the information related in Samuel that Saul's body was impaled on the walls of Beth Shan, the major city in the eastern Jezreel overlooking the Jordan (1 Sam. 31:10). There it was in plain sight of the citizens of Jabesh Gilead, a Transjordan town that lay less than ten miles to the southeast. Having heard of Saul's fate, men from Jabesh Gilead retrieved his body and those of his sons and gave them proper burial in their own city. Their solicitous and compassionate spirit without doubt reflected the gratitude of these good people for Saul's having rescued them from Ammonite siege, his first deed of military conquest nearly forty years before (1 Sam. 11:1–11). Another explanation of their concern, perhaps a far deeper explanation, is that the people of Jabesh Gilead shared kinship with Saul. The tribe of Benjamin from which Saul sprang had suffered near annihilation at the hands of a united Israel because of the injustice accorded the Levite and his concubine (Judg. 19–20). Wives then had to be found for the six hundred Benjamite survivors lest the tribe die out (Judg. 21:6–7). The solution included obtaining women from Jabesh Gilead (Judg. 21:12). In all likelihood, one of these became a forebear of Saul; hence, his unusual interest in and connection to Jabesh Gilead (cf. 2 Sam. 2:4–5; 21:12).

3. The Assessment of Saul (10:13–14)

The tragic end of Israel's first king is explained by the chronicler as resulting from (1) disobedience of the clear word of the Lord and (2) an effort to seek that word in an illegitimate way, through a medium (the witch of Endor; 1 Sam. 28:7). In succinct and pointed language the historian concludes that the Lord slew Saul and turned the kingdom over to David. The two are not unrelated, of course, for David all along had been the "man after his [God's] own heart" (1 Sam. 13:14) whose succession was a foregone conclusion long before Saul's death (1 Sam. 15:26; 16:13, 14). Saul's death, the result of his rebellion, provided the immediate and practical means of Davidic succession.

B. The Succession of David (11:1–12:40)

The establishment of David's rule over all Israel at Hebron receives but scant attention from the chronicler (11:1–3) compared to the account of Samuel with its intrigue, formed and broken alliances, and intense struggle for dominance (2 Sam. 2:1–5:5). In fact, the historian here entirely omits the seven-and-one-half-year reign of David at Hebron over Judah alone and plunges immediately into his rule over the entire nation. Clearly, his interest is in showing that David's succession to Saul was universally endorsed, even by the tribes (including Benjamin) over which Saul had been king.

Likewise, David's choice and conquest of Jerusalem as capital appears as almost a routine and uncomplicated matter (vv. 4–9). The native population of Jebusites, an Amorite people (cf. Josh. 10:5), at first resisted but finally fell to a strategem whereby Joab secretly entered the city (v. 6; cf. 2 Sam. 5:8) and allowed the Israelites access. David then took up residence at Zion, the fortress of the city, which thereafter bore the name "City of David" (v. 7). Around Zion, David built other structures extending across to the older city Jebus (or Mount Ophel). This joined the supporting terraces (or Millo, from the Hebrew verb meaning "to fill") of Zion with the defensive walls of Jebus (v. 8). Joab was responsible for the restoration of the remainder of the city.

Having identified Joab as commander-in-chief because of his exploits in taking Jerusalem, the chronicler further supports the powerful kingship of David by listing the remainder of his mighty men. The first of these are the chiefs, two of whom appear here by name. There were three in all as the chronicler implies (v. 12), the third, Shammah, being named in 2 Samuel 23:11–12. These made up the level of authority directly under Joab, David's own nephew (cf. 1 Chron. 2:16). As for the two mentioned by the chronicler, Jashobeam (Josheb-Basshebeth in 2 Sam. 23:8), chief of the officers (or of the "thirty" or "three" [LXX]), was famous for slaying 300 enemy soldiers at one time (v. 11) in a conflict otherwise unrecorded. Eleazar, the second chief, was celebrated because he had fought along with David at Pas Dammim (perhaps Ephes Dammim in 1 Sam. 17:1) and had achieved a significant victory over the Philistines (vv. 12–14). This battle, too, is otherwise unknown. Shammah apparently also participated in this campaign (2 Sam. 23:11–12).

A second group of these heroes distinguished themselves by penetrating the defenses of the Philistines (who then occupied Bethlehem) and bringing to David a flask of water from the well of his hometown (vv. 17–18). So moved was David by this show of self-sacrificing loyalty, he could not drink the water but poured it out as an offering to the Lord (v. 19). The occasion was David's conflict with the Philistines in the Rephaim Valley after he had become king at Hebron and before he took Jerusalem (2 Sam. 5:17–25; cf. 2 Sam. 23:13–17).

These three warriors are unnamed but probably included Abishai (v. 20) and Benaiah (v. 22). Abishai, a brother of Joab (cf. 1 Chron. 2:16), was chief of this group because of his valor in slaying 300 men but he did not gain the ranks of the first three (cf. 2 Sam. 10:9–10). Benaiah prevailed over man and beast in single-handed conflict (vv. 22–23) but also never gained the first rank during David's kingship, though he became captain of the guard. Solomon, however, promoted him to commander-in-chief following Joab's disloyalty at the time of Solomon's accession to Israel's throne (1 Kings 2:35).

The chronicler next lists "the mighty men" (vv. 26–47), apparently the "thirty" of verse 30 plus an extra list of sixteen (vv. 41–47) not named in the parallel roster of 2 Samuel 23:24–39. By considering several of the names prior to verse 34 as "sons of Hashem," there are exactly thirty names in the list, Asahel and Uriah inclusive (vv. 26–41). Samuel, however, has a total of thirty-seven (2 Sam. 23:39). This is reached by including the three of the first rank (vv. 8–12), the two of the second rank who are named (vv. 18–23), and thirty-two in the list that parallels the list of thirty in Chronicles. The Samuel and Chronicles registers do not agree exactly, though most of the differences are in spelling. Other variations may be due to different times of composition so that some individuals were replaced by others, by regarding "sons of Hashem" (1 Chron. 11:34) as two unnamed men, and the like. "The thirty" was likely a technical term referring to a military unit that might or might not have exactly that number at any given time.

To confirm further the unanimous support David enjoyed from both Israel and Judah, the historian relates events in David's career from his days of flight from Saul to his coronation over all Israel at Hebron and makes the point that the people, without tribal distinction, had affiliated with him. This first occurred at Ziklag, the Philistine city David occupied as a fiefdom during his last months of flight (12:1–7; cf. 1 Sam. 27:1–7). Amazingly enough, many of the bowmen and slingers who joined him there were defectors from Saul's own tribe of Benjamin, twenty-three of whom are named in the passage. Eleven others came from Gad (vv. 8–15) to David's desert stronghold (i.e., Adullam; cf. 1 Chron. 11:15–16). These brave warriors from east of the Jordan crossed the river at the flood stage (v. 15; cf. Josh 3:15) so eager were they to press the battle against those who occupied the valleys through which they passed westward. Others joined them, notably men of Benjamin and Judah, whose leader Amasai (perhaps the same as David's nephew Amasa; cf. 1 Chron. 2:17; 2 Sam. 19:13) pledged their loyal devotion to David in light of God's clearly revealed will (v. 18).

Men of Manasseh became allies of David when he was about to participate with the Philistines in their final drive against Saul at Gilboa (vv. 19–22; cf. 1 Sam. 29:1–3). Though they stopped short of undertaking this because of Philistine suspicions, they returned to Ziklag with David and helped him overtake and defeat the Amalekite predators who had sacked Ziklag in David's absence (1 Sam. 30).

In a final statement affirming David's favorable reception by all Israel on the occasion of his coronation at Hebron, the chronicler lists the delegations that attended, noting that every tribe was represented (vv. 23–27). This obviously followed the negotiations that had been undertaken by Abner and others (cf. 2 Sam. 3:17–21; 5:1–3) to bring Israel under David's dominion for these contingents had come "to turn Saul's kingdom over to him" (1 Chron. 12:23). The figures for each tribe total over 300,000, an immense display of Israelite solidarity.

The whole affair culminated in a three-day festival with food and drink provided by the joyful celebrants from near and far (vv. 38–40). And those in attendance were only typical for the chronicler notes that "all the rest of the Israelites were also of one mind to make David king" (v. 38).

C. The Movement of the Ark (13:1–14)

The coronation of David as king over Israel and Judah and his selection of Jerusalem as the political capital prompted him to take the next step—namely, to make Jerusalem the religious center as well. This required the construction of a tabernacle and the return of the ark as its centerpiece.

For reasons far too complex to rehearse here, it seems that the movement of the ark took place late in David's reign and not at the beginning as Chronicles suggests. The placing of the narrative here, then, accords with thematic and theological concerns, not chronological. A commentary must deal with the text and context as they stand, however, so the following discussion will make no attempt to reconstruct the account along chronological lines.

David's concern is to gather a great assembly from throughout the land to celebrate the return of the ark, which, he says, had been inaccessible to him and the people through all the years of Saul's reign (vv. 1–3). In fact, the ark had been captured by the Philistines about 1100 B.C. (1 Sam. 4:11), had remained in Philistine hands for several months (1 Sam. 6:1), and then rested at Beth Shemesh briefly (1 Sam. 6:13–15) and at Kiriath Jearim for over one hundred years (from 1100 until some years into David's reign, which began in Jerusalem in 1004 B.C.).

David's appeal met with resounding success, and a throng gathered from as far south as the Shihor River on Egypt's border (perhaps even one of the eastern Nile branches; cf. Josh. 13:3; Isa. 23:3; Jer. 2:18) and from as far north as Lebo Hamath (perhaps Lebweh on the Orontes). Then with their king they went to Baalah, another name for Kiriath Jearim (v. 6; cf. Josh. 15:9), some eight miles west of Jerusalem. They there retrieved the ark, which functioned not only as the respository of the stone tablets of the covenant (cf. Exod. 25:21) but as the symbol of the presence of the divine Name (v. 6), that is, of God himself (cf. Deut. 12:5, 11; 14:23–24; etc.).

Disregarding the clear instructions of the Law concerning the handling of the sacred ark (Exod. 25:13–14; cf. 1 Chron.

15:2, 13, 15), the priests and Levites placed it on a cart and started out from the house of Abinadab, its custodian (cf. 1 Sam. 7:1), to Jerusalem with great celebration (vv. 7–8). At Kidon (a personal or place name not otherwise known) the load shifted and the ark would have fallen to the ground had not Uzzah reached out to prevent it. His impiety on top of the irregularity of the ark's transportation brought God's judgment on Uzzah and he died (v. 10).

This tragic turn of events gave rise to a new name for the place—Perez Uzzah ("outbreak against Uzzah"). David, terrified by the results of his sacrilege, left the ark nearby at the home of Obed-Edom for three months, a fact that brought great blessing upon him and his descendants (cf. 1 Chron. 26:4–5).

D. The Establishment of David's Rule (14:1–17)

Among the trappings and signs of power in the ancient Near Eastern world were the construction of public buildings— particularly palaces and temples—the acquisition of wives and children, and victories over enemies. All three of these are apparent in David's reign and the chronicler points them out as a token of God's favor upon him and the nation (vv. 2, 17).

First, Hiram King of Tyre sent materials and craftsmen to build a palace and other structures suitable for a king (v. 1; cf. 2 Sam. 5:11; 1 Kings 5:1). Next is the account of the wives David married in Jerusalem (v. 3) and the list of children he had by them (vv. 4–7). This list adds two names to that of 2 Samuel 5:14–16 (Elpelet and Nogah) and calls the next-to-last son Beeliada rather than Eliada. The genealogy of 1 Chronicles 3:5–8 agrees with that of chapter 14 except for variations in spelling.

The third hallmark of successful kingship was military conquest so the historian relates two anecdotes among many he could have cited as evidence of God's favor. The first of these (vv. 8–12) describes the same battle as that underlying the brief pericope of 1 Chronicles 11:15–19 (see above). The Philistines had attempted to prevent David's acquisition and control of Jerusalem and so had launched a preemptive attack in the valley of Rephaim, between Jerusalem and Adullam (cf. 2 Sam. 5:17– 21). David, having sought divine guidance (v. 10), counterat-

tacked and achieved a smashing victory. The Philistines were so
stunned that they left their idols behind to be burned (v. 12), an
ironic twist to the victory by the Philistines over a century
earlier in which the ark of the Lord had been captured from
Israel (1 Sam. 4:11). The victory by David was commemorated
by the naming of the battlefield Baal-Perazim, "the Lord who
breaks out" (v. 11).

Undaunted, the Philistines made another effort at Rephaim
(vv. 13–16). This time the Lord directed David to set an ambush
and to attack when they heard the wind blowing through the
balsam trees as the sound of marching feet. The tactic, effectively employed, forced the Philistines to flee once more, this
time from Gibeon to Gezer, a distance of fifteen miles.

E. The Arrival of the Ark and Its Installation (15:1–16:43)

Having completed his governmental building projects,
David erected a tabernacle to house the ark (v. 1). Mindful of
the carelessness with which he had undertaken the transportation of the ark before (13:7–13), this time he made certain that
everything was according to the specification of the law of
Moses (vv. 2–15). Zadok and Abiathar, chief priests of the lines
of Eleazar and Ithamar respectively, were in charge along with
the heads of the three Levitical clans: Uriel of Kohath (v. 5),
Asaiah of Merari (v. 6), and Joel of Gershom (v. 7). Three other
Kohathite leaders—Shemaiah of Elizaphan (cf. Exod. 6:22),
Eliel of Hebron (cf. Exod 6:18), and Amminadab of Uzziel (cf.
Exod. 6:18)—lent their support (vv. 8–10) and priests and
Levites together consecrated themselves to accomplish the task
in an appropriate manner (vv. 14–15).

The Levitical musicians likewise participated according to
their clan associations (vv. 16–24). Heman, a Kohathite and
grandson of Samuel (cf. 1 Chron. 6:33); Asaph, a Gershonite
(1 Chron. 6:39); and Ethan, a Merarite (1 Chron. 6:44), led the
procession with bronze cymbals (v. 19). Next came eight
instrumentalists playing lyres according to ălāṁoth (a musical
term; cf. Ps. 46 title) followed by six others playing harps
according to shĕmînîth (cf. Ps. 6 title). Kenaniah, an expert in
vocal music, was next (v. 22). The ark itself evidently followed
Kenaniah preceded and followed by two doorkeepers at each

end (vv. 23, 24). Somewhere between them was a unit of seven priests playing the trumpets.

David himself appears to have led the procession into Jerusalem, dressed like the priests and Levites in the sacred robe and ephod of linen (v. 27). Along the way and in response to the blessing of God the officiants offered sacrifice of seven bulls and seven rams (v. 26). The only thing that marred the event was the revulsion of Michal, David's wife, at what she perceived to be David's shameful lack of decorum (v. 29; cf. 2 Sam. 6:20). What actually troubled her, no doubt, was David's role as priest, something for which her own father had been punished (1 Sam. 13:8–13). Also, David's triumphal entry into the city with the ark marked finally and unmistakably the end of the old order of Saul and the beginning of the new one of David.

When at last the ark rested in the tent David had prepared for it, he led in the offering of burnt offerings and fellowship offerings, blessed the assembly, and distributed to them bread and cakes of dates and raisins (vv. 1–3). The sharing of such food was appropriate to the ceremony of fellowship offerings (cf. Lev. 7:11–14; Deut. 27:7). To ensure the continuation of the proper care and use of the ark and tabernacle David appointed certain Levites to attend to them from then on (vv. 4–6). These were led by Asaph and included most of the men who earlier appeared in the list of musicians (15:19–24). Their principal responsibility, then, was to lead in the praise of the Lord in music (v. 4). To provide a model of such praise David compiled a psalm of thanksgiving, which he committed to Asaph for the occasion and for time to come (v. 7).

This psalm (vv. 8–36), as most scholars recognize, consists of parts of three others, which must, therefore, have already been in existence. First Chronicles 16:8–22 finds parallel in Psalm 105:1–15; 16:23–33 in Psalm 96:1b–13a; and 16:34–36 in Psalm 106:1b-c, 47–48. The exposition of these psalms and thus of this composite may be found in the commentary on Psalms in this series.

There was more to the worship of the Lord at the tabernacle than music, of course, so Asaph, in charge of the whole, had assistants to oversee these other aspects. Obed-Edom (probably the same as Obed-Edom the Gittite, 1 Chron. 13:13–14), a second Obed-Edom, the son of Jeduthun (cf. 1 Chron. 15:24), and Hosah (cf. 1 Chron. 26:10) were among these, the latter two being gatekeepers.

Meanwhile, the old Mosaic tabernacle of Shiloh remained functional at Gibeon, having arrived there probably after the slaughter of the priests at Nob by Saul (1 Sam. 21:1–6; 22:19; 1 Chron. 21:29). Since there is no indication that the new tabernacle of David at Zion rendered the other obsolete or illegitimate (to the contrary, Solomon worshiped the Lord at Gibeon; 1 Kings 3:4–10), it is obvious that a line of priests must also officiate there. This, then, accounts for the parallel order of priests, that descended from Eleazar headed by Zadok and that descended from Ithamar headed by Abiathar (v. 39; cf. 1 Chron. 15:11).

The Gibeonite shrine was served not only by Zadok and his fellow priests but by Heman, the son of Joel and grandson of Samuel (cf. 1 Chron. 15:17), and Jeduthan (also known as Ethan, 1 Chron. 6:44; cf. 15:17), not to be confused with the father of Obed-Edom the gatekeeper (v. 38). These were in charge of music and the keeping of the gate (v. 42).

F. David's Concern for a Temple (17:1–27)

Sometime after David had completed the construction of his palace and had moved the ark of the Lord into its new tabernacle on Mount Zion, he was struck with the stark contrast between the two structures and implied to Nathan that he wished to replace the tent with a temple, a solid and impressive building more appropriate to his God (v. 1, cf. v. 4). The Lord responded through the prophet that he had been content hitherto to dwell in tents and had never sought anything more permanent (vv. 5–6). Indeed, rather than David's desire and futile efforts to magnify the Lord, the Lord would magnify him!

He had already raised him from being a follower of sheep to a leader of men (v. 7). He had delivered him from his enemies and now would exalt his name (i.e., his reputation) among the rulers of the earth (v. 8). More than that, he would establish his people Israel in the land so solidly that they would never be moved. This eternal nation would be under the dominion of David and his descendants after him, particularly that son who would build the temple in David's place (vv. 9–12). Though this is clearly a reference to Solomon (1 Chron. 28), the eternal duration of his reign requires a fulfillment that transcends a merely human agent (v. 14).

The response of David to this remarkable revelation is of utmost theological importance (vv. 16–27). He had, of course, understood the promises of God concerning a chosen people, a chosen land, and a dynasty of kings that would culminate in one single, messianic ruler (cf. Gen. 12:1–3; 17:1–8; 49:10; Exod. 19:4–6; Num. 24:17; 1 Sam. 2:10). He also came to know that he stood in that line of kings as its founder (1 Sam. 13:14; 15:28; 16:1, 12–13; 23:15–18) and that in him and through him God had established his rule upon the earth (Ps. 2:6–7; 89:3–4; 110). Later prophets would speak of David's kingship and would connect it to a scion of David, a Messiah, who would fulfill the terms of this Davidic covenant (cf. Isa. 9:6–7; 11:1–5; Jer. 30:4–11; Ezek. 34:23–24; 37:24–25; Amos 9:11–15).

In spite of the promises already known to David, he was amazed that he could be the recipient of such divine grace (1 Chron. 17:16–18). Only the God of Israel, the unique One who had redeemed his people and made them his own possession, could accomplish what he had pledged (vv. 20–23). Such a God was worthy of undying praise for his promise was sure and his covenant rule would endure forever (vv. 24–27).

G. David's International Relations (18:1–20:8)

1. The Philistines and Moabites (18:1–2)

The defeat of the Philistines appears to be limited to the conquest of Gath and its immediate surroundings. The parallel account (2 Sam. 8:1) says that David took Metheg Ammah ("the bridle of the mother [city]"). It is likely then that this enigmatic reference is clarified by the chronicler and is a way of designating Gath, the Philistine city closest to Israel.

As for Moab, the narrator says only that David defeated it and brought it into subjection as a tributary state. By contrast, the author of Samuel (2 Sam. 8:2) speaks of a brutal massacre in which two out of every three Moabites were slaughtered. It is clearly the intention of the chronicler, in line with his well-established canons, to simply take note of David's positive achievements and to spare the reader the grisly and (to him) unnecessary details. Moreover, David's own roots lay partially in Moab by virtue of his descent from his Moabite great-grandmother Ruth (cf. Ruth 4:13, 17). The heinousness of David's rage against Moab has no place in the chronicler's sympathetic account.

2. The Arameans (18:3–11)

The campaigns of David against the Arameans seem to be connected to the Ammonite wars that commenced shortly after David began to reign at Jerusalem (cf. 19:1–19). The Arameans had come to the assistance of the Ammonites, a move that brought David's massive retaliation (19:16–19). Hadadezer (Hadarezer in Heb.) king of Zobah, a state north of Damascus, was first to suffer at David's hands because of his hostilities against Israel. Having gone east of the Euphrates to secure reinforcements (v. 3; cf. 19:16), he left his rear unprotected so David pursued his troops as far north as Hamath, 100 miles north of Damascus. The result was the capture by Israel of 1,000 chariots, 7,000 charioteers, and 20,000 infantrymen.

The second phase of David's Aramean wars developed out of the first (vv. 5–8). Hadadezer, after suffering the debacle at Hamath, enlisted help from Damascus, but to no avail. This time the enemy suffered 22,000 casualties and the kingdom of Damascus became a tributary state. In addition David took spoil from Hadadezer in the form of gold shields and bronze objects from the cities of Tebah (or Tibhath; Betah in 2 Sam. 8:8, NASB, KJV), Cun (not mentioned in Sam.), and Berothai (not mentioned here, but cf. 2 Sam. 8:8), places known now in Egyptian texts and lying northeast of Baalbek. These objects, the narrator says, were melted down and provided bronze for articles in Solomon's temple (cf. 1 Chron. 29:2).

The third recorded encounter between David and Aram was more peaceful, for when Tou king of Hamath learned what had befallen his Aramean allies, he sued for peace (vv. 9–10). Since he also had been at war with Hadadezer, Tou welcomed the defeat of the king of Zobah and the opportunity to forge a friendly alliance with David. This he did by sending his son

Hadoram (Joram in 2 Sam. 8:10) to Jerusalem with lavish gifts of gold, silver, and bronze (v. 10). These, too, David dedicated to the Lord as indeed he had done with all his spoils of war (v. 11).

3. The Edomites (18:12–13)

In a campaign against Edom in the Valley of Salt (the Wadi el-Milḥ just east of Beersheba) Abishai, nephew of David (cf. 1 Chron. 2:16; 11:20), administered a crushing defeat. This so completely overwhelmed Edom that Israel established garrisons throughout the country and brought it under tribute. The chronicler's account is somewhat surprising because he credits Abishai and not David with victory over Edom, particularly since the author of Samuel attributes it to David (2 Sam. 8:13–14). Moreover, the title of Psalm 60 says that Joab slew Edom in the Valley of Salt, the number of the dead being 12,000 (not the 18,000 of Chronicles). The resolution may lie in the fact that Abishai was in general command and that his brother Joab, serving under him, was responsible for two thirds of the casualties (cf. 1 Kings 11:14–16).

4. David's Administration (18:14–17)

The chronicler's reference to "Abishai son of Zeruiah" (18:12) may have called to his mind "Joab son of Zeruiah" (v. 15) and thus the major officials of the royal court. These included Joab, the chief military officer (cf. 11:6); Jehoshaphat son of Ahilud, the recorder (i.e., keeper of the archives); Zadok and Ahimelech son of Abiathar, the priests (Abiathar having been temporarily replaced; cf. 1 Kings 2:27, 35); Shavsha (Seraiah in 2 Sam. 8:17), the secretary (or scribe); Benaiah, commander of the Kerethites and Pelethites (an elite, probably Philistine, troop; cf. 1 Sam. 30:14; 2 Sam. 15:18; 20:7; 1 Kings 1:38, 44), and David's sons who were among his top officials. Second Samuel 8:18 describes David's sons as kōhănîm (usually translated "priests"), so Chronicles may be helpful in suggesting a meaning for this word other than "priest" since David's sons (except possibly for Solomon; cf. 1 Chron. 1:3–9) could not be priests in light of their non-Levitical ancestry.

5. The Ammonites (19:1–20:3)

David's wars with the Ammonites took place quite early in his reign as is clear from the fact that Nahash king of Ammon, whose death was the occasion for David's overture toward Nahash's son, was king in Saul's earliest years (1 Sam. 11:1). This was at least fifty years prior to the events of this narrative (40 years of Saul's reign plus 7 of David's at Hebron plus whatever years had passed already in Jerusalem).

Since Nahash had showed kindness toward David in some unspecified way (v. 2), David responded by sending a message of congratulations and goodwill to Hanun, Nahash's son, upon his accession to the throne of Ammon (v. 2). Hanun's advisers misinterpreted David's motives, however, and counseled Hanun to send the Israelite delegation back to Jerusalem in shameful humiliation (v. 3). This they did by shaving them and shortening their garments to a most immodest length (vv. 4–5).

The Ammonites were not long in learning that they had offended David intolerably so they hired Aramean mercenaries to fight with them against what they knew would be massive Israelite retaliation (vv. 6–9). These came from Aram Naharaim (upper Mesopotamia; cf. Gen. 24:10; Judg. 3:8), Aram Maacah (between Damascus and the Sea of Galilee), and Zobah (cf. chap. 18:3–5 and comments). In all, there were 32,000 chariots and charioteers (evidently from Aram Naharaim and Zobah) besides the king of Maacah and his troops, presumeably infantry.

This host marched south to Medeba (now known as Madaba), some twenty miles southwest of Rabbah. The Ammonites then left their city of Rabbah, pressing the invading Israelites between themselves and the Arameans (v. 10). Joab, consistent with the military strategy appropriate to such a situation, divided his troops. He sent his brother Abishai against the Ammonites at Rabbah, while he led his men against the Arameans in the open field. If either one were in danger of defeat, he said, the other should come to his aid. With confidence in God they struck (vv. 14–15). The Arameans immediately retreated, the disheartened Ammonites withdrew to their fortified city, and Joab returned to Jerusalem.

The Arameans, however, sent for reinforcements from beyond the River (i.e., the Euphrates), a force commanded by Shophach (v. 16; cf. 18:3). David rose to this new challenge, met the Arameans head on (at Helam, 40 miles east of the Sea of Galilee, according to 2 Sam. 10:16), and forced them to submit (v. 17). The Arameans lost 7,000 charioteers (2 Sam. 10:18 has 700), 40,000 infantry, and all the lands under Hadadezer's control. Never again were the Arameans willing to take sides with Ammon (v. 19).

At the turn of the year Joab resumed the Ammonite campaign and this time was successful in breaching and capturing the city of Rabbah (20:1). The chronicler notes that David remained in Jerusalem but omits the narrative of his adultery with Bathsheba, which took place at this time (cf. 2 Sam. 11:1–5). This was well-known, of course, and did not need to be repeated. Furthermore, it would not contribute to the chronicler's desire to enhance the Davidic monarchy.

The account is further abbreviated by lack of information as to how David came in possession of the crown of Ammon's king, a great ceremonial object of gold, which weighed one talent (ca. 75 pounds). Samuel points out that the capture of Rabbah was not achieved at once. The siege undertaken by Joab (2 Sam. 11:1) was followed by David's adultery and his murder of Uriah (11:14, 17). After all that, the city fell. David was present, said Joab, for it was important that the king be given credit for such an achievement (2 Sam. 12:28). Thus, the chronicler could speak of David's personal involvement in the fall of Rabbah and the savage reduction of Ammon and its people (20:3).

6. The Philistines (20:4–8)

The chronicler begins (18:1) and ends his account of David's wars by speaking of the Philistines for no enemy occupied so much of David's attention or proved as intractable as these. The parallel passage 2 Samuel 21:15–22 includes one conflict—David's hand-to-hand combat with Ishbi-Benob (vv. 15–17)—that the chronicler omits, probably because David appears to be weak and almost incompetent. There are three other episodes, however, that both include.

The first of these describes a battle at Gezer (Gob in 2 Sam.

21:18) in which Sibbecai the Hushathite (one of the 30 heroes; cf. 11:29) killed Sippai, a Rephaite giant (v. 4). The Rephaite were apparently indigenous to the Transjordan region and were noted for their remarkable physical stature (cf. Deut. 2:10–11, 20–21). They may have been employed by the Philistines as mercenaries or Rephaite (that is, Anakite) elements may have settled among the Philistines (Josh. 11:21–22).

A second engagement (which 2 Sam. 21:19 also locates at Gob) consisted of a duel between Elhanan son of Jair and his victim Lahmi the brother of Goliath (v. 5). Second Samuel 21:19 identifies Elhanan as the son of Jaare-Oregim of Bethlehem and says that his foe was Goliath himself. The second of the list of thirty heroes is also Elhanan, but his father is Dodo of Bethlehem (1 Chron. 11:26). This Elhanan is probably not the same as the other (and certainly not to be identified with David). The Elhanan who was son of Jair (Jaare-Oregim is just a variation) may have slain both Goliath and his brother Lahmi. Moreover, there must have been at least two Goliaths, one killed by David and the other by Elhanan, since the David-Goliath contest took place many years earlier before David was king. There is also the possibility that there is a textual defect in 2 Samuel 21:19 and that "Lahmi the brother of" dropped out at some time or other before the name Goliath. The chronicler's version would, therefore, be the complete and more accurate rendition.

The third Philistine conflict (vv. 6–8) resulted in the death of a mutant giant at the hands of Jonathan, son of David's brother Shimea (Shammah in 1 Sam. 16:9). This narrative brings to a conclusion the accounts of David's incessant troubles with the giant descendants of Rapha at Gath (v. 8; cf. v. 4 and comments).

H. David's Census and Its Aftermath (21:1–22:1)

Late in David's reign, probably after Absalom's rebellion and perhaps in response to it (cf. 2 Sam. 24), David commanded Joab to number the fighting men of Israel and Judah (vv. 1–8). This was done, the chronicler says, at the instigation of Satan (v. 1). The author of Samuel, however, attributes it to the Lord himself (2 Sam. 24:1). Theologically, there is no inconsistency between the accounts for God controls the actions of Satan ultimately and even uses him to accomplish his purposes (cf. Job 1:12; 2:6; 1 Kings 22:19–23). Consistent with the chronicler's tendency to protect the reputation of the Lord and his king, it is no surprise that he emphasizes the agency (Satan) and not the cause (God) of David's act.

The reason for the census is not clear but it came about in connection with God's displeasure with his people (2 Sam. 24:1). The census then became the occasion for the Lord to punish the people for whatever they had done and in itself constituted an act of sin on David's part (1 Chron. 21:8). That sin obviously was David's failure to recognize that God's power and not human armies was the secret of military and political success (v. 3).

The total sum of fighting men was 1,100,000 in Israel and 470,000 in Judah (v. 5). This did not include the tribe of Levi for the men of that tribe were exempted from military service (cf. Num. 1:47–49). It also omitted the Benjamites, apparently because the procedure was interrupted before Joab reached that tribe (1 Chron. 27:24). The figures here are quite different from those of the parallel account of 2 Samuel 24:9. There the total of Israelites is 800,000 and of Judeans 500,000. Various explanations for the differences have been proposed but most likely perhaps is the suggestion that Samuel counts only the conscripts of Israel, not the regular army, which may have numbered about 300,000 (cf. 1 Chron. 27:1–15). The chronicler reached his total by adding the two. On the other hand, the chronicler counted only the conscripts of Judah, failing to include a standing army of 30,000 for which there is some evidence (2 Sam. 6:1). Samuel's figure of 500,000 would be the total of both groups.

In response to David's sin, the Lord offered him three choices of punishment: three years of famine, three months of enemy pursuit, or three days of plague at the hand of the angel of the Lord (vv. 9–12). Rejecting the second option, David cast himself upon the Lord's mercy. This resulted in the third judgment, the unleashing of a terrible plague, which cost Israel 70,000 lives (v. 14).

Just as the affliction was about to strike Jerusalem itself, the Lord interrupted the angel who was then standing at the threshing floor of Araunah the Jebusite. Throughout Old Testament literature, the phrase "angel of the Lord" connotes the Lord himself, either present in an incarnation or other bodily form or as represented by an angelic messenger (cf. Gen. 16:13; 18:1-2; 22:11-12; 48:16; Judg. 6:16, 22; 13:22-23; Zech. 3:1). The fact that he accepts worship and yet (as in our passage) stands independent of God (vv. 15-17, 18, 27-28) leads many Christian scholars to identify him as a person of the Godhead, perhaps the preincarnate Jesus Christ.

When David and the elders saw the angel standing with drawn sword and about to destroy Jerusalem they fell down on their faces before God. Confessing that it was he and not his people who had brought this awful visitation, David prayed that the wrath of the Lord might not be indiscriminate but might fall only on him and his family (v. 17). Graciously God heard his prayer and commanded him to build an altar on the threshing floor so that he might offer an appropriate sacrifice.

The threshing floor, located just north of the city, was a level, ledgy area where grain could be spread to be trampled underfoot by oxen or other beasts (v. 20) and then winnowed by the late afternoon breezes from the West. This one belonged to Araunah (otherwise unknown), a member of Jerusalem's original Jebusite population.

Having received the command to build an altar, David approached Araunah to enter negotiations for the purchase of the threshing floor. Araunah had already seen the angel of the Lord and realized thereby the sacredness of the moment and place. When David drew near, the Jebusite fell on his face before him in deference to his king but also because of the vision of the angel. So impressed was he with all that he had seen, Araunah refused David's offer to buy the threshing floor at full price. Instead he wished to offer it as a gift and to provide his own threshing oxen as sacrifices for the altar David would build. His threshing sledges would provide fuel for the sacrificial fire and his wheat a grain offering (v. 23).

Impressed as he must have been by this magnanimous gesture, David declined because it would not be right, as he said, to "sacrifice a burnt offering that costs me nothing" (v. 24). David had brought the plague upon his people as he had freely confessed (v. 8). He must now offer at his own expense those sacrifices that represented his own repentance and remorse and that were appropriate for the occasion. He therefore paid the enormous sum of 600 gold shekels (about 15 pounds of gold) for the threshing floor, built an altar, and offered burnt offerings and fellowship offerings in accordance with the requirements of the Law (v. 26; cf. Lev. 9:22–24). As a sign of his forgiveness and acceptance, the Lord "answered him with fire from heaven" (v. 26), exactly as he later responded to Elijah on Mount Carmel (1 Kings 18:38). Thus, the plague ended and Jerusalem was saved (v. 27).

The account of this episode in 2 Samuel 24:18–25 agrees up to this point with the chronicler's version except for the price David paid for the threshing floor. Samuel says that the amount was 50 shekels, not 600. What must be carefully noted, however, is that the threshing floor and oxen alone cost 50 shekels (2 Sam. 24:24), whereas Chronicles includes in the sale the site of the threshing floor (1 Chron. 21:22), an area of many acres.

The chronicler's rendition helps to prepare the way for the fact that Solomon's temple was built on this very property (cf. 2 Chron. 3:1). Its size and space for its attendant facilities would require a considerable amount of land. Samuel, in fact, omits any reference to the threshing floor as the site for the temple, but the last section of 1 Chronicles 21 provides this anticipation (vv. 28–30). The tabernacle of Moses with its great altar of sacrifice was at Gibeon (cf. 1 Chron. 16:37–40 and comments), but David would not sacrifice there for fear of God's wrath (v. 30). This must mean that the theophany in the form of the angel of the Lord was a sign that a transition was occurring. Worship no longer would be focused on the central sanctuary at Gibeon but on the new one that Solomon would build in Jerusalem. To go back to the old place after God had showed his approval of the new (vv. 26, 28) would invite divine displeasure and judgment.

That this is David's interpretation of the encounter at the threshing floor is clear from 1 Chronicles 22:1 for he makes the astounding observation that "the house of the LORD God is to be here, and also the altar of burnt offering for Israel."

For Further Study

1. Why did the chronicler give so much less attention to the reign of Saul than the author of 1 Samuel?

2. Why was the chronicler concerned to demonstrate that David was well received by all Israel, not just Judah, on the occasion of his coronation at Hebron?

3. Account for the chronicler's emphasis on the Davidic tabernacle, the ark, the priesthood and Levitical orders, and David's plans for the temple. How did the religious structure relate to the monarchy?

4. What is the theological significance of David's conquests over surrounding enemy nations? How can such military activity be harmonized with the biblical notion of "peace on earth"?

5. Explain the function of the threshing-floor of Araunah (i.e., Mount Moriah) as a holy place. What is the biblical view of the presence of God among his people in special places?

Chapter 3

The Preparation for Succession
(1 Chronicles 22:2–29:30)

A. David's Preparation for the Temple (22:2–19)

Though David was expressly forbidden to build a temple (1 Chron. 17:4), he did undertake preparations for its construction, including the purchase and development of a site (22:1). Moreover, he had collected precious metals and other materials as spoils of war and had set these aside to be used for the temple and its furnishings (cf. 1 Chron. 18:7–8, 11). He now conscripted stonecutters from among the alien population of Israel (v. 2) and provided iron for the manufacture of nails, bronze in huge quantities, and cedar timbers from Phoenicia (vv. 3–4). All this he did because Solomon was so young and inexperienced he could not be expected to do it on his own (v. 5).

Neither Samuel nor Kings makes any reference to David's extensive preparations for the temple though they certainly were very much aware of them. Though not anti-David in their attitude, they saw no importance in this preliminary work. Their interest was in the construction itself—something that did not take place until after David's death (cf. 1 Kings 5:1–5).

True to the chronicler's purposes, which have surfaced over and over thus far, he wishes to glorify David in every way possible. Thus, even the temple construction depended on the preparations that David had made. Here one can see how theological constraints affect the way that historical events are preserved in the various accounts.

Sensing that his years were limited, David commenced the

process of royal succession by a series of charges, addresses, and instructions that would guarantee a smooth transition. He first addressed his son Solomon concerning the covenant promises and responsibilities which he would inherit and the role that the temple would play in their implementation (vv. 6–16).

He rehearsed with him how he had desired to build the temple and how that dream had been frustrated (vv. 6–7). As a warrior who had shed much blood, he was disqualified for such a peaceful pursuit (v. 8). Rather, his son, whose very name means peace (Heb. šĕlōmō, "peace"), would bring it to pass (vv. 9–10a). The warlike character and activity of David may indeed have been incompatible with the nature of temple building, but it is also possible that David's preoccupation with war was a necessary prerequisite to the peace that made temple building possible. The man of war, therefore, paved the way for the man of peace (cf. 2 Sam. 7:9; 1 Chron. 22:18).

Solomon, this man of peace, would not only build the temple but would be the son of God whose dynasty would reign forever (v. 10). This bold statement is in line with others concerning David himself. Psalm 2, for example, refers to the king as God's son (v. 7), a thought picked up by the author of Hebrews who quotes this psalm in support of the divine sonship of Jesus Christ (1:5; 5:5). That this son is exclusively human as well is evident from the original statements of the Davidic covenant in which dire consequences follow the disobedience of any of David's royal descendants (2 Sam. 7:14). Solomon, then, is the son of God in a human, adoptive sense, but another son of David, Jesus the Christ, was Son of God in the fullest and divine sense (cf. 1 Chron. 17:16–27 and comments).

Continuing his charge, David urged Solomon to be fastidious in his obedience to the Lord (v. 11) and to seek God's wisdom in keeping all the demands of the Law (vv. 12–13; cf. 2 Chron. 1:10). To do this is to bring the success of the Lord (v. 13).

Finally, David took inventory of the provisions he had gathered for the temple (vv. 14–16). These included 100,000 talents of gold (3,750 tons), one million talents of silver (37,500 tons), bronze and iron without limit, and abundant supplies of timber and stone. In addition, there was an adequate supply of skilled laborers and craftsmen for every aspect of the project (v. 15).

To ensure that his young son received all the encouragement possible, David ordered the leaders of Israel to lend their full support (vv. 17–19). The Lord was with them, he said, and the land was at rest and ready for such an undertaking. All that was required was submission to the will of God and dependence on his mighty power. Until the job was done, the ark and all the accoutrements of proper worship could not find their proper resting place.

B. David's Preparation of Religious and Political Personnel (23:1–27:34)

1. The Levites in General (23:1–24:31)

More than temple building was necessary for a smooth transition of government. David, therefore, made careful arrangements for the structures of religious and political life by appointing leadership personnel who would carry on under the new administration that would follow his death.

First, of course, was the solid entrenchment of his son Solomon as king (23:1). The selection of Solomon as successor had been made from the time of Solomon's birth (cf. 22:9–10), but that selection did not go unchallenged as the account in 1 Kings especially makes clear (1 Kings 1:5–10). The rebellion of Absalom (2 Sam. 15–18) alerted David to the need to solidify his choice of Solomon so he set in motion a co-regency whereby Solomon's appointment was made public some time before his actual coronation. This appointment is in view in this passage whereas the succession to sole regency does not come about until some months later (1 Chron. 29:22–23; cf. 1 Kings 1:33–34, 38–40).

With a passing word concerning the other leaders (v. 2), the chronicler next addresses the matter of the organization and assignments of the Levites. A head count revealed that there were 38,000 of them from thirty-years-old and upward (v. 3; cf. Num. 4:3). Of these 24,000 were to be involved in the direct ministry of the temple, 6,000 were to be officials and judges over outlying areas (cf. 1 Chron. 26:29–32), 4,000 were gatekeepers, and 4,000 were musicians. All these David divided into three courses according to their descent from Gershon, Kohath, or Merari (v. 6).

The Gershonites (vv. 7–11) consisted of two clans, those descended from Ladan (or Libni; 1 Chron. 6:17) and those from Shimei. Jehiel, Zetham, and Joel (v. 8) evidently were distant offspring of Ladan who became leaders in David's time. Another individual named Shimei was ancestor of the three other Levites contemporary with David: Shelomoth, Haziel, and Haran (v. 9). The line of the other Shimei, the son of Gershon, resulted in four "sons," two who produced their own families and two who combined their small families to make one. Thus, the Ladanites contributed six houses of Levites and the Shimeites three.

The Kohathites (vv. 12–20) gave rise to the priests through Aaron, son of Amram (v. 13). Amram's other son was Moses whose descendants were not priests but Levites. Moses' two sons, Gershon and Eliezer, produced Shubael and Rehabiah respectively, the latter having many sons of his own (v. 17). The Shebuel (or Shubael; 1 Chron. 24:20) and Rehabiah families were the two Kohathite groups to whom David gave assignment.

Other Kohathites came from the line of Izhar, only one family, that of Shelomith, being represented here. The descendants of Hebron, third son of Kohath, were four families (v. 19) and those of Uzziel two more. This makes a total of nine Kohathite families set apart by David.

The Merarites (vv. 21–23) were represented by Eleazar and Kish, sons of Mahli (v. 21), and Mahli, Eder, and Jeremoth, sons of Mushi (v. 23). Eleazar died without sons so his daughters married their cousins, the sons of Kish. This meant that the descent of Mahli resulted in one family and that of Mushi three for a total of four families. All three Levitical clans contributed twenty-two families in all to the service of the temple.

Even this great number of families and individuals (38,000; v. 3) was evidently insufficient for the task because David was forced to reduce the minimum age requirement from thirty to twenty (vv. 24, 27). Also he seems to imply that the older, more reliable men were not so necessary in light of the fact that the temple, unlike the tabernacle, did not need to be transported and its furnishings handled with such care (vv. 25–26). This deviation from the age standards of the Torah (Num. 4:3) was initiated by David without any apparent challenge (1 Chron. 23:27; cf. 2 Chron. 31:17) and suggests that he, as theocratic leader and intermediary, had the authority to make such changes.

The duties of these Levites involved such matters as the care of the courtyards and various rooms of the temple; the purification of sacred objects and furnishings (cf. Num 3:31); the preparation of the show bread, meal offerings (Lev. 6:20), and other baked goods; and participation in the morning and evening services of praise (v. 30). They also tended to the offering of burnt offerings on the Sabbath, new moon festivals, and other stated feasts.

In summary, the chronicler says that the Levites appointed by David carried out their responsibilities faithfully as they pertained to the Tent of Meeting, the Holy Place, and the temple (v. 32). "Tent of Meeting" here (as opposed to temple) presupposes the transitional period between David and Solomon when the temple was not yet standing and the Davidic tabernacle was still in use.

Having identified the twenty-two Levitical families and their general duties, the chronicler turns to their relationship to the lines of the priests and to their assignments by family within those relationships (24:1–31).

There were only two divisions of priests, of course, since two of Aaron's sons died early in their ministries (Lev. 10:2). This left the lines of Eleazar and Ithamar, the former traced out in detail earlier by the chronicler (cf. 1 Chron. 6:4–15). Because there were two sanctuaries in need of priestly service in David's time (cf. 1 Chron. 21:28–22:1), it was necessary that both orders of the Aaronic priesthood function simultaneously. This is why David divided up the priests under the headship of Zadok at Gibeon and Ahimelech at Jerusalem.

The link between Eleazar and Zadok is well established (6:4–15). Between Ithamar and Ahimelech there lacks a full genealogical bridge, but it certainly finds support in the fact that Ahimelech was son of Abiathar (v. 6) who was in turn son of another Ahimelech (1 Sam. 23:6), one who traced his lineage back to Eli through Ahitub (1 Sam. 22:11) and Phinehas (1 Sam. 14:3). Moreover, Samuel's warning that the priesthood of Eli would yield to another line (1 Sam. 2:35), a warning fulfilled in the replacement of Abiathar by Zadok (1 Kings 2:35), shows clearly that Abiathar's son Ahimelech was of the line of Ithamar.

In the course of dividing the priests by family, it became clear that the descendants of Eleazar outnumbered those of Ithamar two to one. There were sixteen in the order of Eleazar and only eight in Ithamar's. So as not to have all the families of one order serve in succession, lots were drawn to determine the sequence in which each would officiate. The legitimacy of both lines of priests is clear from the statement that "there were officials of the sanctuary and officials of God" from both sets of families (v. 5). The better translation of that clause might be "there were officials of the sanctuary, that is, officials of God" to distinguish these leaders from the political leaders to be described later.

Shemaiah the scribe recorded the names of the families of priests and took note of the order in which they would serve (v. 6). It seems that the two orders served alternatively and since that of Eleazar had twice as many families as did Ithamar, the latter families must have served twice as often as the others.

Since it seems clear that the order of Eleazar drew first (v. 6), the first man in the following list, Jehoiarib, must be an Eleazarite. The even numbers up through sixteen, then, would be of the order of Ithamar. Unfortunately, most of the names in the list appear only here so it is impossible to identify them by order. It may be that Abijah of the eighth lot (v. 10) is the ancestor of Zechariah, father of John the Baptist (Luke 1:5). If so, Zechariah was of the line of Ithamar. The names Jehoiarib and Jedaiah (v. 7) occur together also in 1 Chronicles 9:10 (cf. Neh. 7:39) to refer to priests who returned from Babylonian Exile. This makes it likely that the names in the present list are not only names of individuals but of priestly families (or orders) as well.

Following the assignment of the priests by lot, David and his assistants divided up the Levites similarly (vv. 20–31). The Kohathites were first, followed by the Merarites. For some reason the Gershonites do not appear here (but cf. 23:7–11).

The Amram clan (vv. 20–21) was represented by the family of Shubael and his son Jehdeiah (who does not appear in the previous list; cf. 23:16) and the family of Rehabiah and his son Isshiah (also not named before). The Izhar clan (v. 22) offered the family of Shelomoth and his son Jahath. The Hebron clan (v. 23) presented four families and the Uzziel clan (vv. 24–25), the families of Micah and his brother Isshiah and their sons Shamir and Zechariah.

There were two previously identified clans of Merari, Mahli and Mushi, and a third, Jaaziah, that appears only here (v. 26). The families from Jaaziah (v. 27) were Beno, Shoham, Zaccur, and Ibri. Those from Mahli (vv. 28–29) were Eleazar (with no descendants; v. 28) and Kish, whose son was Jerahmeel. The Mushi clan (v. 30) was represented by the families of Mahli, Eder, and Jerimoth. The casting of the lot assured that all of these would serve in their turn with no preference given to any above another (v. 31).

2. The Levitical Musicians (25:1–31)

The chronicler previously drew attention to the important role of the Levites in the ministry of music in the tabernacle services (1 Chron. 15:16–24) and he listed the principal leaders, particularly Heman, Asaph, and Ethan (v. 17). He now addresses that same ministry in the context of the preparations for temple building and worship.

Of special interest is the fact that the allocation of function for these Levites was in the hands of David and the "commanders of the army" (25:1). The close connection between music and the military, though surprising perhaps, may reflect the long-standing Israelite tradition of holy war. When Joshua led the armies of Israel against Jericho, he did so with the ark of the Lord and the accompaniment of music (Josh. 6:8–11).

On the other hand, the Hebrew underlying "commanders of the army" (śārê haṣṣābā') might better be rendered "chiefs of the serving host" or something similar, since the context has otherwise established that David and various other cultic officials had undertaken the task of assigning lots and responsibilities (24:3, 31). Reference to the military at this point would be most intrusive and without adequate explanation. Finally, the word *śar* ("chief," "official") also occurs in 1 Chronicles 24:5 to refer to the religious leaders of Israel descended from Eleazar and Ithamar. It may be these to whom the chronicler refers in 25:1.

The ministry of these musical Levites was to prophesy either through or accompanied by music (v. 2). That music was closely connected to Old Testament prophetism is very clear (cf. 1 Sam. 10:5–6; 2 Kings 3:15) but the manner in which the music contributed to the prophesying is not. What must be kept in mind is that prophesying more often than not consisted of proclamation and not prediction or even reception of divine revelation. To prophesy frequently entailed the singing of the praises of the Lord precisely as was done in the psalms of Levites, such as Asaph (cf. Pss. 50, 73–83).

The division of the Levites was according to their affiliation with Asaph, Heman, and Jeduthun (or Ethan, cf. 15:17) respectively. There were four sons of Asaph who, with their father, prophesied as the king himself instructed (v. 2). This suggests the leading role the Davidic kings played in the organization and function of the cult. The six sons of Jeduthun (v. 3; cf. v. 17) prophesied under their father's direction and particularly with the use of the harp. Finally, the fourteen sons and three daughters of Heman (vv. 4–6) served the worship by the playing of cymbals, lyres, and harps. These twenty-four (or twenty-seven with Heman's daughters) together with their kin totaled 288 (v. 7). This reflects twenty-four orders of Levites with twelve individuals in each (cf. vv. 9–31).

The four sons of Asaph—Joseph, Zaccur, Nethaniah, and Jesarelah (or Asarelah, v. 2)—appear in lot 1 (v. 9), 3 (v. 10), 5 (v. 12), and 7 (v. 14) respectively. The six sons of Jeduthun are distributed as follows: Gedaliah, lot 2 (v. 9); Izri (or Zeri, v. 3), lot 4 (v. 11); Jeshaiah, lot 8 (v. 15); Shimei (not mentioned before), lot 10 (v. 17); Hashabiah, lot 12 (v. 19); and Mattithiah, lot 14 (v. 21). Finally, the sons of Heman and their order were Bukkiah, lot 6 (v. 13); Mattaniah, lot 9 (v. 16); Azarel (or Uzziel, v. 4), lot 11 (v. 18); Shubael (or Shebuel, v. 4), lot 13 (v. 20); Jerimoth, lot 15 (v. 22); Hananiah, lot 16 (v. 23); Joshbekashah, lot 17 (v. 24); Hanani, lot 18 (v. 25); Mallothi, lot 19 (v. 26); Eliathah, lot 20 (v. 27); Hothir, lot 21 (v. 28); Giddalti, lot 22

(v. 29); Mahazioth, lot 23 (v. 30); and Romamti-Ezer, lot 24 (v. 31).

This pattern is of interest because it shows that the allocation was not purely random. The sons of Asaph had positions 1, 3, 5, and 7; those of Jeduthun had 2, 4, 8, 10, 12, 14; and the Ethanites, the rest. Except for the break in the pattern required by a son of Ethan in position 6, the first two families had alternative assignments up through 8. Then the second two families alternated from position 9 through position 15. All the remaining lots (16–24) were occupied by Ethanites. The purpose of the lots, then, was only to determine in which order the sons of the respective families were to serve within the structure of alternation created by David and his assistants.

3. The Levitical Gatekeepers (26:1–19)

There were four divisions of these: that of Meshelemiah (vv. 1–3), that of Obed-Edom (vv. 4–5), that of Shemaiah (vv. 6–9), and that of Hosah (vv. 10–11). The last descended from Merari (v. 10) and the other three from Kohath as the family affiliations make clear.

Meshelemiah (or Shelemiah, v. 14) was a Korahite descendant of Asaph (or Ebiasaph; cf. 1 Chron. 9:19; Exod. 6:24) and thus a Kohathite (Exod. 6:18, 21, 24). He had seven sons who served with him as gatekeepers (v. 3) and eleven other relatives who must have collaborated with him in other ways (v. 9).

Obed-Edom, whom God had blessed in some special way (v. 5), had eight sons who served with him. The note concerning God's blessing might suggest that this Obed-Edom is the very one in whose house the ark remained en route to Jerusalem from Kiriath Jearim (1 Chron. 13:14). That Obed-Edom, however, is more likely the individual mentioned as one of the two special gatekeepers who attended the ark (1 Chron. 15:17–18, 21, 24; 16:5, 38a). The Obed-Edom here is without doubt the son of Jeduthun since elsewhere, as here (v. 10), he is associated with Hosah (1 Chron. 16:38b), another gatekeeper.

An objection to this may be that Jeduthun (the same as Ethan; cf. 1 Chron. 15:17; 25:1) is a Merarite (cf. 1 Chron. 6:44), while the Levite here is a Kohathite (26:4) if, indeed, Obed-Edom is one of the Korahites introduced in 26:1. This objection has no validity if the Jeduthun of 1 Chronicles 16:38b (the father of Obed-Edom) is a different individual by that name—a distinct possibility.

A branch of the Obed-Edom family was that of Shemaiah (v. 6; cf. v. 8) whose six sons and relatives also served as gatekeepers. All the Obed-Edom descendants connected with this service were sixty-two in number (v. 8).

Hosah, a Merarite, headed a family of four sons who were gatekeepers along with nine other relatives (vv. 10–11).

The assignment of the gatekeepers, like that of the musicians, was by lot (vv. 12–13). Shelemiah (or Meshelemiah, v. 1) was responsible for the east gate (cf. 1 Chron. 9:17–18). His son Zechariah (cf. v. 2; 9:21) was in charge of the northern gate. Obed-Edom and his sons supervised the south gate and storehouse (probably the treasuries of v. 20) respectively. Shuppim (otherwise unknown) and Hosah were stationed at the west gate and the Shalleketh Gate (otherwise unknown).

In sum, there were six gatekeepers day-by-day at the east gate (the most important), four at the north, four at the south, and four at the west (vv. 17–18). In addition, two guarded the storehouse on the south and two others the court by the west gate. The total of twenty-two gatekeepers per day would be the leaders only since there were four thousand gatekeepers in all (1 Chron. 23:5).

4. The Levitical Treasurers (26:20–28)

In addition to the gatekeepers and closely related to them in responsibility were Levites in charge of the storehouses. The term here for "treasury" (Heb. *'ôṣār*) is different from that used in 26:15, 17 (*'asōph*) but the words are synonyms that denote a place for the keeping of any objects or materials. There are two of them here, one for the "house of God" and one for the "dedicated things." The former refers to a storage area for sacred furnishings already prepared for use in the temple (cf. 1 Chron. 9:28–29; 23:28–29), while the latter describes one for the housing of spoils of war David and others had appropriated for later use in the temple (vv. 26–28).

The Hebrew text indicates that Ahijah was over both treasuries (v. 1), but the Septuagint (followed by the NIV) follows a better tradition in reading the personal name Ahijah as a short form of a word to be rendered "fellow," thus "their fellow Levites." This relieves the problems of double leadership of the treasuries and the sudden emergence of an otherwise unidentified Ahijah.

The treasury of the temple was under the jurisdiction of descendants of Ladan, a Gershonite. He is the same as Libni (cf. 1 Chron. 6:17; 23:7–8), son of Gershon. Specifically in charge were Jehieli (Jehiel in 23:8) and his two sons Zetham and Joel (v. 21).

The treasury of the dedicated things was in the hands of Kohathites and in particular those who traced their descent through Amram, Moses, and Gershom. Shubael appears to have had overall supervision (v. 24) but Shelomith and his relatives, who in turn were related to the line of Shubael through Eliezer (v. 25; cf. 23:15–17), were directly in charge (vv. 26, 28). They were to protect and otherwise superintend the spoils of war that had come to Israel from the days of Samuel to the present hour (vv. 26–28; cf. 1 Chron. 18:7–8, 11; 22:3–5; 29:2–5).

5. Other Levitical Officials (26:29–32)

Kohathite Levites through the clan of Amram managed the treasury of the dedicated things as the foregoing has shown (vv. 24–28). Other Kohathites of the clan of Izhar had the task of serving as officials and judges outside the capital, presumably still in religious and temple affairs (cf. Neh. 11:16). Kenaniah and his sons had the oversight of this work (v. 29).

The clan of Hebron provided 1,700 leaders under Hashabiah for other matters of cult and state west of the Jordan (v. 30). In the Transjordan the same work fell to Jeriah, another Hebronite, and his 2,700 followers. All these arrangements, the chronicler says, were made by David in his very last year (v. 31; cf. 23:1). The officials and judges of Hebron on both sides of the Jordan total 4,400. The 6,000 of 1 Chronicles 23:4 may represent these plus those under Kenaniah (v. 29) and those in Jerusalem proper.

6. Military and Political Officials (27:1–24)

The standing army of Israel under David consisted of twelve divisions of 24,000 men each (v. 1). Each division served for one month in rotation and each apparently corresponded to tribal or provincial jurisdictions (thus "head of families" in v. 1; cf. 1 Kings 4:7–19). These monthly assignments no doubt represented active duty in times of peace or only minor conflicts. Most likely other divisions or the entire army could be called up as the situation required.

The division of the first month was commanded by Jashobeam son of Zabdiel (vv. 3–4). He was the first name in David's list of heroes (1 Chron. 11:11), having slain 300 at one time. His descent from Perez would make him a Judean if this Perez is the son of Judah.

Dodai the Ahohite was captain of the second division (v. 4). His son Eleazar was the second of David's heroes (1 Chron. 11:12). The fact that he has an assistant, Mikloth, might imply that he was aged and unable to assume leadership on the field.

The third division was led by a Levite, Benaiah son of Jehoiada the priest (vv. 5–6). He is identified by the chronicler as the Benaiah who was a leader of the Thirty, being numbered among the second group of the Three (1 Chron. 11:22–25). He later became commander of Israel's armies under Solomon (1 Kings 4:4). His assistant was his own son Ammizabad.

Division four was under the leadership of Asahel the brother of Joab, David's nephew (1 Chron. 2:15–16). He too was a mighty man but he did not achieve a rank among the first or second Three (1 Chron. 11:26). His assistant was his son Zebadiah.

The fifth division was under Shamhuth (Shammoth in 11:27), called here an Izrahite (v. 8). The chronicler elsewhere knows him as the Harorite (11:27) and the author of Samuel calls him the Harodite (2 Sam. 23:25), obviously a textual variation. The resolution may lie in his being from Harod and of the family of Zerah of Judah (Zerahite is virtually the same as Izrahite in Hebrew), though the only place by this name is in northern Israel (cf. Judg. 7:1).

Ira was commander of the sixth division (v. 9). His linkage

with Tekoa suggests that he too was a Judean for Tekoa lay twelve miles south of Jerusalem.

The seventh captain was an Ephraimite, Helez the Pelonite (v. 10). Another of David's heroes, Ahijah (1 Chron. 11:36), is also called a Pelonite. What this means is unclear but in light of the previous "Tekoite" (v. 9) it must refer to a place name such as Pelon (see also "Paltite" of 2 Sam. 23:26).

In the eighth month Sibbecai the Hushathite was in command (v. 11). Hushah was a Judean (1 Chron. 4:1–4) so once again a leading military figure comes from that tribe. Moreover, Sibbecai was one of the thirty heroes (1 Chron. 11:29), a warrior who distinguished himself by slaying a Philistine giant (2 Sam. 21:18; cf. 1 Chron. 20:4).

Abiezer, leader of the ninth division, was a Benjamite from Anathoth, the priestly village on the outskirts of Jerusalem (v. 12). He, too, appears in the list of David's thirty mighty men (2 Sam. 23:27; 1 Chron. 11:28).

Maharai the Netophathite, another Judean by descent through Zerah (v. 13), was in charge of division ten. Netophah was a small town in the vicinity of Bethlehem. Like Abiezer, Maharai was in the heroes list (2 Sam. 23:28; 1 Chron. 11:30).

The division of the eleventh month was that of Benaiah the Pirathonite of the tribe of Ephraim (v. 14). Clearly different from Benaiah son of Jehoiada (v. 5), who was a Levite, this one appears in the list of Thirty (1 Chron. 11:31; 2 Sam. 23:30). "Pirathonite" indicates that he (like Abdon the judge; Judg. 12:13) was from the village of Pirathon, five miles south of Samaria.

The twelfth and last unit was under the command of Heldai the Netophathite (v. 15). Like his fellow officer Maharai (v. 13), he was from the Judean hill country. His name appears as one of the Thirty heroes in 1 Chronicles 11:30 as Heled (and in 2 Sam. 23:29 as Heleb). Of interest is his descent from Othniel, Israel's first judge.

The list that follows that of the twelve divisions and their commanders appears to be one of a more political nature (vv. 16–24). The "officers" (Heb. *nāgîd*) here exercise leadership over the tribes and their distinctive tribal areas and apparently they do so simultaneously and permanently. One should note that though there are twelve tribes listed (plus the priestly community, v. 17), Asher and Gad are not. Their absence is made up by the inclusion of Levi (v. 17) and by considering East Manasseh (v. 21) and West Manasseh (v. 20) as two tribes. Moreover, Simeon, which normally falls within Judah as an assimilated tribe, is counted separately here (v. 16). Historically, the omission of Asher and Gad may be accounted for by the domination and/or occupation of their areas by the Phoenicians and Ammonites respectively (cf. 2 Sam. 17:27–29).

Most of the names of the tribal officials cannot be further identified but some can. Zadok, leader of the Aaronites (i.e., the priests), is none other than the high priest who served the tabernacle at Gibeon (1 Chron. 16:39) before becoming the priest at Solomon's temple (1 Kings 2:35). Elihu (v. 18), brother of David and leader of Judah, is the same as the Eliab of 1 Samuel 16:6.

The chronicler associates the list of leaders with David's census (vv. 23–24; cf. 1 Chron. 21:1–8) suggesting perhaps that these leaders were in place at the time of census and that they participated in it. He adds the information here that the vast sums of men counted (1,100,000 in Israel and 470,000 in Judah; 1 Chron. 21:5) did not include any under twenty years of age nor was the tally complete since God's preemptive wrath precluded the counting of Levi and Benjamin (21:6).

7. Miscellaneous Officials (27:25–34)

A royal court and centralized government as large and sophisticated as David's grew to be in his last years required an elaborate bureaucracy with clearly specified areas of responsibility. The royal storehouses (v. 25), to be differentiated from the "treasuries for the dedicated things" (26:20), housed the assets of the national government (that is, of the king himself). This probably consisted of such things as precious metals (cf. 1 Chron. 29:3–5) and goods and produce in kind. The treasury in Jerusalem was under the supervision of Azmaveth, while those throughout the country were under Jonathan son of Uzziah.

Ezri son of Kelub was responsible for field crops (v. 26), Shimei for the vineyards (v. 27), and Zabdi for the wine and wine cellars. The olive and sycamore-fig industry was in the hands of Baal-Hanan (v. 28), while Joash supervised the production of oil. The care of the herds of the lush pastures of Sharon fell to Shitrai (v. 29), and the herds that grazed elsewhere were under the watchful eye of Shaphat. Obil the Ishmaelite, affiliated as he was with these desert peoples, was an appropriate administrator of the camel economy. The oversight of the donkeys was entrusted to Jehdeiah (v. 30). Finally, the management of the flocks was the responsibility of Jaziz.

Higher officials yet were Jonathan, David's uncle (Heb. *dôd* might better be "kinsman" in general; cf. 2 Sam. 21:21), who was a counselor and scribe. Jehiel was evidently some kind of adviser to David's sons (v. 32). Ahithophel was also counselor to the king (v. 33). If, as seems likely, this is the same Ahithophel as the one who defected to Absalom (cf. 2 Sam. 15:12, 31), the chronicler's note here must refer to an earlier time before that defection for Ahithophel ended up a suicide several years before the setting of these lists (2 Sam. 17:23).

In fact, the counselors at the end of David's life must have been Jehoiada son of Benaiah and Abiathar (1 Chron. 27:34), individuals otherwise unknown but identified here as successors to Ahithophel. Hushai, special confidant of the king, does appear, however, in an earlier narrative and precisely with reference to Ahithophel (2 Sam. 15:32–37). It was his duty to return to Jerusalem from David and to counter the counsel Ahithophel offered to Absalom. Having accomplished this objective (2 Sam. 17:14–15), Hushai passed off the scene until the cursory note of the chronicler.

Last in the list is Joab, commander of the royal army (27:34), a position he had occupied all through David's reign and on into the period of Solomon's succession (1 Kings 2:28–35).

C. David's Great Assembly (28:1–29:22a)

1. Encouragement to Build the Temple (28:1–10)

Having presented a detailed summation of all of David's religious and political structures and the personnel attached to them (cf. 23–27), the chronicler now recounts the story of the great assembly to which they all were invited (28:1). David's life was rapidly drawing to a close (23:1) so it was urgent that he put in motion all that was important to a smooth dynastic succession, not least of which was preparation for the temple (cf. 1 Chron. 22:17–19).

Rising to his feet, David addressed the throng by first of all reminding them of his desire to build a temple for the Lord, a privilege that was denied him (vv. 2–3). Long ago God had chosen the tribe of Judah as the source of Israelite kingship (cf. Gen. 49:10), the house of Jesse as its mediator (1 Sam. 16:1), and David as its first and chief example (1 Sam. 16:12). It was now time for the kingship to pass to the next generation, a move already initiated by the Lord (v. 5) and put in motion by David (1 Chron. 23:1b). It was this son who must build the temple, a fact made possible by virtue of Solomon's having been chosen, as had David, to be the son of God (v. 6; cf. 17:13; 22:10). The building of the temple would be a tangible affirmation of the stability and permanence of the rule of David and his royal descendants if they obeyed the requirements of the covenant arrangement (v. 7; cf. 1 Chron. 17:11–14; 2 Sam. 7:13–17).

Following the rehearsal of the covenant promises, David charged first the people (v. 8) and then Solomon (vv. 9–10) to be obedient to the stipulations that were incumbent upon them as God's chosen ones and to set about the work of temple construction. Solomon must acknowledge and serve the Lord if he expected blessing. Failure in these areas would result in rejection by the Lord, a casting off that would last forever.

2. The Pattern of the Temple (28:11–19)

David could not build the temple but he had collected the building materials (1 Chron. 29:2–5) and now presented to Solomon in writing (v. 19) and probably in drawing the most detailed specifications as to its execution. This, he said, came not from his own imagination or that of any other man but from the revelation of God by his Spirit (vv. 12, 19). The earthly temple, then, was to be nothing less than a replica of a heavenly temple or at least of a heavenly ideal (cf. Exod. 25:40; Acts 7:44; Heb. 8:2, 5). This is why every part as well as the whole must be made in accordance with the explicit pattern God had revealed. These parts included the portico, various side and upper chambers (cf. 1 Kings 6:5–6), the large inner chamber ("its inner rooms," cf. 1 Kings 6:17–18; 2 Chron. 3:5–7), and "the place of atonement" (v. 11; i.e., the Most Holy Place; cf. 2 Chron. 3:8–9).

The revelation of the Spirit also extended to the construction of the temple courts and buildings in support of the temple, such as the treasuries of the temple of God and of the dedicated things (v. 12; cf. 1 Chron. 26:20). Even the instructions for temple service—the personnel and objects to be used—came by heavenly revelation (vv. 13–18). Nothing could be left to chance because in every detail the plan, purpose, and meaning of the Lord was to be apparent.

3. A Final Word of Exhortation (28:20–21)

In words typical for such occasions of transition (cf. Josh. 1:6–9; 1 Chron. 22:13), David encouraged Solomon to undertake what had been committed to him in the full knowledge of the presence and enablement of the Lord. All was now ready, he said, and Solomon had only to call upon the human and material resources available to him.

4. The Requests for Gifts (29:1–9)

Continuing his address to the assembly, David spoke concerning the need for the leaders and the people to involve themselves in providing materials necessary for the temple construction. Theirs was an especially important contribution because Solomon was young and inexperienced, therefore unable to give mature leadership, and the temple as the house of God demanded gifts that far exceeded normal construction requirements (v. 1).

He had already collected and set aside precious metals and stones as well as wood, most of which came from military conquest (cf. 1 Chron. 18:7–8, 11; 22:3–5, 14–16). Now he made lavish gifts of his own personal resources because of his devotion to the temple of the Lord (v. 3). These consisted of 3,000 talents (ca. 110 tons) of gold from Ophir (cf. 1 Kings 9:28; 10:11; 22:48; 2 Chron. 8:18; 9:10), a land in South Arabia fabled for its precious metals, and 7,000 talents (ca. 260 tons) of refined silver. All this was for the paneling of the temple walls and for other projects requiring their use (vv. 4–5).

After detailing his own commitment to the work, David asked who else among them would be willing to do likewise (v. 5). Without hesitation the leaders responded affirmatively and among them gave 5,000 talents (ca. 190 tons) and 10,000 darics (ca. 185 pounds) of gold, 10,000 talents (ca. 375 tons) of silver, 18,000 talents (ca. 675 tons) of bronze, and 100,000 talents (ca. 3,750 tons) of iron (vv. 6–7). In addition, those who had precious stones donated them to the safekeeping of Jahiel the Gershonite, supervisor of the temple treasury (cf. 1 Chron. 23:8; 26:21). Such overwhelming generosity on the part of all these officials brought great joy to both the people and the king (v. 9).

5. David's Prayer and Dedication (29:10–22a)

The climax of the convocation was a song of praise, composed no doubt for the occasion (vv. 10–13), followed by a prayer of confession and petition (vv. 14–19).

After recognizing the Lord as the father of Israel (v. 10), David extolled his power, his glory, and his sovereignty over all things (v. 11). From him came all blessings (including wealth to lavish on the temple) so he is deserving of the thanks of his people (vv. 12–13).

In his prayer David confessed that he and his people could give nothing without the beneficence of the Lord (v. 14). They were mere mortals, utterly dependent upon him for even the ability to give to the work of the temple (vv. 15–16). He and the people had been willing to give, David said, but even that willingness was from God (v. 17) and could continue only as the covenant God of their fathers renewed it from one generation to the next (v. 18). For Solomon especially David prayed, beseeching the Lord to give him a spirit of devotion and obedience in the task of building the temple (v. 19).

Following the prayer, David invited the assembly to join him in praising the Lord, a request they honored by falling prostrate before both the Lord and the king (v. 20).

The next morning David led the assembly in a massive sacrifice of burnt offerings consisting of 1,000 bulls, 1,000 rams, and 1,000 male lambs together with drink offerings and other sacrifices (that is, thank or peace offerings; cf. Num. 15:1–10). Their eating and drinking in the presence of the Lord (v. 22a) symbolized the covenant setting of their gathering (cf. Exod. 24:5–11).

D. The Succession of Solomon (29:22b–30)

On an earlier occasion (1 Chron. 23:1) David had designated Solomon as his heir apparent, a move that must have resulted in Solomon's being elevated to co-regent with his father. This interpretation of events follows from the fact that all of the careful organization of the religious and royal leadership described in 1 Chronicles 23–27 followed Solomon's appointment, a process that presupposes considerable time. Moreover, the assembly of 28:1 is obviously different from that of 23:1–2 because the personnel involved are different. Finally, and most important, the chronicler notes that the assembly acknowledged Solomon as king "a second time" (1 Chron. 29:22b), and this time the recognition was followed by anointing. The only other reference to Solomon's anointing is in 1 Kings 1:38–40, the setting of which must be on the morning following the great assembly described in 1 Chronicles 28:1–29:20. While the sacrifices described in 1 Chronicles 29:21–22a were being offered then, the movement to interdict the succession of Solomon (1 Kings 1:5–31) was already underway. This explains why David so hastily arranged the anointing of Solomon to succeed him (1 Kings 1:32–34; cf. 1 Chron. 29:22b). The reference to the anointing of Zadok is also common to both sources (1 Kings 2:35; 1 Chron. 29:22b) and supports the sequence of events proposed above.

Solomon sat in the place of his father and enjoyed the support and obedience of his Israelite subjects (vv. 23–24). Neither Saul nor David knew the royal splendor that came to Solomon from God's gracious hand (v. 25).

The chronicler concludes his account of David's reign (vv. 26–30) by citing its length of forty years (seven in Hebron and thirty-three in Jerusalem), by remarking on the long and prosperous life of the king, and by asserting once more his succession by Solomon (vv. 26–28). Then, in a note of special interest to historiography, he refers to his historical sources and other documents containing material pertinent to David's life and reign. These include the records of Samuel (perhaps 1 Sam. 1–24), Nathan, and Gad (possibly 1 Sam. 25–1 Kings 2:12). His own account up to this point (that is, 1 Chron.) was based on these and other records though, of course, he shaped and arranged them in accordance to his own special historical and theological purposes.

For Further Study

1. Compared to Samuel and Kings, which say little about David's preparation for temple construction, the chronicler stresses that David did virtually everything except the actual building. Why does Chronicles assign to David such an important role in this project?

2. Account for the centrality of music in the worship of Israel in the temple. What relevance, if any, might this have for church music in terms of both the content and extent of a music ministry?

3. Why is so much attention paid to the ministries of the Levites? Read an article on Levites in a Bible dictionary or encyclopedia. What parallels may be drawn between the temple Levites and contemporary ministries in the church?

4. Why was David so concerned about his succession by Solomon? What might this teach about the integrity and permanence of the Davidic dynasty up to and including Jesus himself?

Chapter 4

The Reign of Solomon
(2 Chronicles 1:1–9:31)

The Book of 2 Chronicles, though separated from 1 Chronicles, is a direct continuation of the latter in the Hebrew manuscripts and ought to be regarded as a part of the whole without interruption. Thus, 1 Chronicles ends with Solomon firmly in place as king of Israel (29:28), and 2 Chronicles begins with that same affirmation (1:1).

A. The Assembly at Gibeon and Solomon's Might
(2 Chron. 1:1–17)

1. The Purpose of the Assembly (1:1–6)

Though David had built a tabernacle on Mount Zion and the ark of God was in it, Solomon did not resort there for this first great religious convocation of his reign. He went to Gibeon, the site of the Mosaic tabernacle. There the great bronze altar of sacrifice built by Bezalel (cf. Exod. 31:11) was located and on it Solomon offered up his thousand burnt offerings (vv. 5–6).

The purpose of the assembly, of course, was to inaugurate the king's reign with a ceremony of covenant commitment (cf. 2 Sam. 5:3; 1 Chron. 12:38–40). Why he went to Gibeon is not so clear, however. The Mosaic tabernacle had been there all through the reign of David and even since the last years of Saul (cf. 1 Chron. 16:37–38 and comments). Yet, there was now a tabernacle in Jerusalem, one that was uniquely holy by virtue of the presence of the ark. Why should the assembly not gather there?

The answer appears to lie in two considerations. First, the argument has already been made that the Davidic tabernacle and the placing of the ark within it were events rather late in David's reign (cf. 1 Chron. 13:1–14 and comments). Perhaps by Solomon's first year the new worship place in its new location was still such a novelty, a break from tradition, that it did not enjoy widespread acceptance. Second, and more likely, Solomon was eager to maintain the unity of the northern tribes with Judah that David had worked so hard to achieve and maintain.

As the leading city of Benjamin, Gibeon was of utmost importance to the followers of the Benjamite Saul and represented a focal point for all the tribes of the north. As just pointed out, it was the center of religious activity as the presence of the Mosaic tabernacle testifies. Of special interest is the account of David's efforts to unify Israel following Saul's death. The chronicler says little about the matter but the Book of Samuel has some interesting things to relate about the role of Gibeon in this period of transition.

It seems that shortly after Saul's death, Abner moved the seat of government from Mahanaim, its temporary Transjordan location, to Gibeon (2 Sam. 2:12). There a delegation of David's men from Hebron met representatives from the government of Saul in an effort to effect a reconciliation based on a contest of champions (2 Sam. 2:13–17). The Judean side prevailed (v. 17) and perhaps the issue of domination over the whole nation could have been decided then and there had David's hot-headed warriors left well enough alone. They turned the tournament into a full-fledged battle, however, thus alienating Abner and the North from David for years to come (2 Sam. 3:1).

A strong resentment by the northern tribes toward David lasted all through his reign (cf. 2 Sam. 19:40–20:2). It is most reasonable that Solomon would do everything in his power to heal this breach and to effect strong bonds of national unity. What better way could he do this than to hold his first great assembly at the Mosaic tabernacle in the Benjamite city of Gibeon?

2. The Gift of Wisdom (1:7–13)

In response to his devotion, the Lord appeared unexpectedly to Solomon to ask him the desire of his heart (v. 7). Recognizing both his own inadequacy and the enormity of the task that lay before him, Solomon asked for wisdom and knowledge (vv. 9–10). The Hebrew word for "wisdom" (hochmâ) denotes discernment or insight, while "knowledge" (maddā') refers to the acquisition of information and its practical application. Without these gifts, Solomon said, he could not rule his people effectively.

The Lord was touched by this unselfish and noble request and promised Solomon that his wish would be granted and then some. He had not asked for wealth, honor, victory, or long life but would get them anyway and to an extent unknown by any other king of Israel before or after him (vv. 11–12). Thus reinforced, Solomon left Gibeon to take up his responsibilities in Jerusalem (v. 13).

3. Solomon's Prominence and Prosperity (1:14–17)

This passage is a summary statement to confirm the promise the Lord had made to Solomon regarding "wealth, riches, and honor" (v. 12). These evidences of blessing were characteristic of the years of his long reign.

Militarily Solomon was powerful with 1,400 chariots and 12,000 horses (or horsemen; Heb. pārāšîm can mean either). These were located in chariot cities, possibly Hazor, Megiddo, and Gezer (1 Kings 9:15, 19), as well as in Jerusalem (v. 14).

The economy so prospered that gold and silver were as common as pebbles, and cedars were as widespread as the sycamore-fig (v. 15). The language is hyperbole, of course, but reflects a time of unparalleled economic development. An important element of that prosperity was Solomon's monopoly in the trading of horses. He imported them from Egypt and Kue (likely the older name for Cilicia in Asia Minor) and sold them to the Hittites and Arameans, presumably at a handsome profit. His selling prices are unknown but he bought Egyptian-made chariots for 600 shekels of silver (ca. 15 pounds) each and horses for 150 shekels of silver (ca. 3 3/4 pounds) each.

B. The Building of the Temple (2 Chron. 2:1–5:1)

1. The Preparations (2:1–18)

The theme of temple building had occupied the chronicler in his discussion of the last days of David's reign (1 Chron. 21:28–29:19) and it dominated David's own concerns in the transfer of rule from him to his son Solomon. It is not surprising, then, that the first recorded undertaking of Solomon once his authority had been established was the construction of the temple.

He first selected 70,000 carriers, 80,000 stonecutters, and 3,600 foremen to provide the manpower (v. 2). Next he engaged the services of Hiram (Huram in the Heb. text), king of Tyre, who had provided men and materials for the erection of David's palace and public buildings (1 Chron. 14:1). The Phoenicians were fabled for their skill and industry in architecture and construction and even though they were pagans they recognized that the God of Israel had inspired this project and that it, therefore, would be successful (v. 12).

Solomon realized that the temple he wished to build for the burning of incense, for the setting forth of the showbread, and for the offering of burnt offerings on all stated occasions must be a magnificent structure because the God of Israel is greater than all other gods (vv. 4–5). This is not an acknowledgment that other gods existed but only that the Lord excelled even the gods of heathen imagination (cf. 1 Chron. 16:25–26).

But any temple, no matter how glorious, would still be inadequate to represent the presence of the Lord (v. 6). All Solomon could do is seek to provide as fitting a place as possible so he urged Hiram to send his very best craftsmen to supervise and collaborate with his own Israelite artisans whom David had already prepared (v. 7; cf. 1 Chron. 22:15–16).

In addition, Solomon needed logs of cedar, pine, and algum (or almug; cf. 1 Kings 10:11–12), the latter being possibly a juniper or sandalwood. His men would work with the Phoenicians to cut the many timbers required. For their labors Hiram's men would receive 20,000 cors (125,000 bushels) of ground wheat, 20,000 cors of barley, 20,000 baths (115,000 gallons) of wine, and 20,000 baths of olive oil (vv. 8–10).

Hiram responded to Solomon's overtures by sending a letter in which he flattered Solomon by pointing out that Solomon's kingship was a token of the Lord's favor upon his people (v. 11). He then acknowledged that the intelligence and discernment of Solomon that prompted him to build the temple and palace was a gift of the God of Israel, creator of heaven and earth (v. 12). This kind of effusive praise of both Solomon and his God was part of the language of diplomacy and should not be taken to mean that Hiram was convinced of the superiority of the God of Israel. Both Nebuchadnezzar of Babylon (Dan. 3:28–4:3) and Cyrus of Persia (2 Chron. 36:22–23) employed similar speech in formal proclamation.

The man Hiram selected to superintend all the work was Huram-Abi, a half-Israelite whose mother was from the tribe of Dan (vv. 13–14; 1 Kings 7:14 describes her as a Naphtalite so she was either a daughter of that tribe living in Dan or vice versa.). He was ideally suited to the task since he was half-Israelite and thus sympathetic to the project and half-Phoenician and thus skilled in its execution. Hiram commended him as expert in all phases of design and production, well able to work with Solomon's own men (v. 14).

Finally, Hiram requested the payment Solomon had promised and said that upon its receipt he would commence the shipment of logs to Jerusalem by way of Joppa, the seaport most accessible and closest (ca. 40 miles) to Jerusalem. From there they would be carried overland to the capital.

In a final note concerning preparation, the chronicler indicates that the work crews previously designated (v. 2) actually were enlisted not from the general population but from the aliens who lived among them. The enormous number of men involved (153,600; v. 17) suggests that there must have been a significant segment of descendants of the indigenous Canaanite peoples occupying a class status subservient to Israelite masters (cf. Josh. 9:22–27; 2 Chron. 8:7–8).

2. The Temple Structure (3:1–17)

The site of the temple had already been designated in the days of David by the appearance of the angel of the Lord at the threshing floor of Araunah the Jebusite (1 Chron. 21:18; 21:28–

22:1). This threshing floor is here more precisely located on Mount Moriah, the hill just north of Jebusite Jerusalem to which Abraham had taken his son Isaac to offer him as a burnt offering to the Lord (Gen. 22:1–2). Thus, the place marking the great act of Abraham's faith became the spot the Lord God chose to represent his presence among his covenant people. The temple mountain and its vicinity thereafter became part of Solomon's greatly expanded city of Jerusalem (cf. 1 Kings 3:1).

So momentous an event was the laying of the temple foundations, its date was recorded so that forever after it might be commemorated. It took place in the fourth year of Solomon's reign, on the second day of the second month of the year. This would be the month Ziv (or April-May; cf. 1 Kings 6:1), 967–966 B.C. The account in 1 Kings 6:1 specifies this as the 480th year after the Exodus thereby dating the Exodus at 1447–1446. The reason the work could not commence in Solomon's first year is clear from the preceding discussion: He had to undertake careful and time-consuming negotiations with Hiram and allow sufficient time to acquire and gather together all the materials for the project. The Kings account relates that the stonework, for example, was done at the quarries so that the construction was largely prefabricated (1 Kings 6:7). This obviously would require a great amount of time.

The foundation of the temple building proper was 60 cubits long by 20 cubits wide (90 feet by 30 feet according to the common eighteen-inch cubit). The portico at the front (on the east side; cf. Ezek. 10:18–19) was 20 cubits long, 10 wide (according to 1 Kings 6:3), and 20 high (so some ancient versions; the Hebrew has 120 [180 feet!], which is clearly out of proportion). First Kings 6:2 adds the information that the temple was 30 cubits (45 feet) high. The entire structure then was 70 cubits (105 feet) long, 20 cubits (30 feet) wide, and 30 cubits (45 feet) high at the temple and 20 cubits (30 feet) high at the portico. One should compare this with the Mosaic tabernacle, which was 30 by 10 by 10 cubits (45 x 15 x 15 feet; cf. Exod. 26:15–37).

The entire interior of the larger chamber was sheathed in gold over a panel of pine. Incised in and attached to the walls were precious stones and decorations of palm trees, chains, and cherubim. The trees may have represented the Tree of Life (cf. Gen. 2:9; 3:20, 22; Rev. 2:7; 22:2, 19), while the cherubim bring to mind those creatures who guarded "the way to the tree of life" (Gen. 3:24). The "chain designs" (v. 5) may, on the basis of the parallel description in 1 Kings, be flower petals or blossoms and gourds (1 Kings 6:18). Their significance is not altogether clear but in line with the palms and cherubim they undoubtedly also refer to the garden setting.

The gold of Parvaim (a place not yet identifiable) must have been most rare and costly (v. 6) for it was selected as the material by which the interior of the Lord's house was covered.

The "main hall" (v. 5) was the so-called Holy Place (cf. Exod. 26:33) as opposed to the Most Holy Place (v. 8), the inner chamber whose dimensions were 20 cubits (30 feet) by 20 cubits. The main hall, then, was twice as long, 40 cubits by 20 (v. 3; cf. v. 8). Since the Most Holy Place of the temple was a perfect cube of 30 x 30 x 30 feet (1 Kings 6:20), it is obvious that it must have been shorter in height than the main hall or Holy Place or that its floor was 15 feet higher in order for the roof level of the entire temple to be uniform. The latter seems more likely for this would elevate the Most Holy Place above the outer chamber in such a way as to suggest the relative height of the presence of God represented by the ark within it.

Like the Holy Place, the interior of the Most Holy Place was plated with gold, 600 talents (23 tons) of it (v. 8). The golden nails alone weighed 50 shekels (1.25 pounds). Most conspicuous were a pair of sculptured cherubim overlaid with gold. These figures, which symbolized the presence of the Lord by their outstretched wings, had a total wingspan of 20 cubits, thus stretching from outer wall to outer wall of the Most Holy Place. The individual wings of each cherub were five cubits long so the spread wings of each touched the wings of the other. Together they stood against the back wall, facing the main hall, so that their wings in effect provided an umbrella over the ark, which stood immediately under and in front of the cherubim. The Hebrew word kĕrûbîm, in fact, means "covering ones" thus describing the function of these creatures: They surrounded the presence of the Lord who dwelled between them (cf. Num. 7:89; Ps. 80:1; 99:1; 2 Chron. 5:7–8).

Between the Holy Place and the Most Holy Place was a linen and yarn curtain of blue, purple, and crimson color. Woven in it were figures of cherubim. Sometimes called the veil, the purpose of this curtain was to partition the whole temple interior into the two rooms so that the most Holy Place particularly could be shielded off from human view (cf. 2 Chron. 5:9).

Two pillars stood in front of the temple, serving a decorative or symbolical function only (vv. 15–17). The chronicler appears to indicate that the pillars were each 35 cubits in height and that each was crowned with a five cubit capital. This would result in columns 40 cubits (60 feet) high. The problem with this is its architectural disharmony with the temple for the pillars would tower over the 45-foot height of the temple by 15 feet. Furthermore, the parallel version of Kings says that each pillar was 18 cubits plus a five cubit capital (1 Kings 7:15–16). This yields a total height of 23 cubits (34 1/2 feet), which would fit the temple height much better.

One may assume, with the New International Version, that the chronicler is adding the heights of the two columns and thus arrives at an approximate of 35 cubits in all (18 plus 18 of Kings) or that an ancient scribe read 35 for 18 in 2 Chronicles 3:15. The reason for his adding the two would be difficult to understand, particularly since such an addition would total 36 and not 35. The figures 35 and 18 in Hebrew can easily be confused, on the other hand (לה = 35, יח = 18), and this possibility appears to offer the better solution, although there is no evidence for such numeral abbreviations so early.

The tops of the pillars (probably the capitals themselves) were decorated by interwoven chains (v. 16) to which were attached a hundred pomegranates. This brief description by the chronicler is greatly augmented by Kings, which says that there were seven chains on each capital and that these interwoven chains were themselves encircled by two rows of pomegranates (1 Kings 7:17–18). There were thus two hundred pomegranates on each capital, a hundred in each row (cf. 2 Chron. 4:12–13). This explains the chronicler's figure of a hundred.

The Book of Kings continues to point out that each capital was carved in the shape of a lily and that the rows of pomegranates circled the lilies above the bowl-shaped part

(7:19–20). Even this more detailed description is difficult to visualize. The best view seems to be that of a 1-cubit-wide band at the bottom of the capital topped by the 4-cubit-tall lily-shaped engraving. The seven-chain embroidery interwoven with the two rows of pomegranates must have covered the band at the base of the capital.

The purpose of the pillars, to say nothing of the symbolism of the chains and the pomegranates, is unclear. What is apparent is the location of the pillars, one to the left (north) and one to the right (south) of the temple entrance, which faced east. The names of the pillars might also give clues as to their significance. The one on the south was Jakin ("he establishes") and the other was Boaz ("in him is strength"). Thus, the pillars spoke of the divine origin and eternal stability of the temple, the monument to the Lord's presence among his people.

3. The Temple Furnishings (4:1–5:1)

The first article in the chronicler's list of temple furnishings is the great bronze altar of sacrifice (v. 1). It measured 20 cubits (30 feet) each way and its height of 10 cubits (15 feet) presupposes steps by which the priests could ascend to make their offerings (cf. Exod. 20:26; Ezek. 43:17). The altar stood in front of the temple, probably before the pillars as well (cf. Exod. 40:6, 29).

The next object was the "Sea of cast metal" (v. 2), which was 10 cubits (15 feet) in diameter, 5 cubits (7 1/2 feet) high, and 30 cubits (45 feet) in circumference. These measurements (which are probably approximations) agree very well with the geometrical equation $C = \pi D$ in which C (the circumference) is 30 cubits, D (the diameter) is 10, and π, of course, is 3.14159. Strict application of the formula would result in a circumference of 31.4159 cubits rather than 30. It is even possible that the dimensions are meant to be taken strictly. In this case, the 31.4159 cubits might be the length of the outside circumference; 30 cubits, the inside (v. 5). In any event, the figures given are in remarkable conformity to mathematical proportions developed by the Greek mathematicians many centuries later.

The huge vessel itself (located south of the altar; v. 10) was decorated with a frieze of two rows of bulls—ten to a cubit in each row—that completely encircled it. Its foundation consisted of twelve other bulls, presumably also cast in bronze (v. 4). Three faced in each direction with their hind quarters toward the center. These supports must have been extremely sturdy for the Sea was a handbreadth thick (ca. three inches). The weight of such an enormous container together with its contents would have been tremendous.

The purpose of the Sea lies in its very name and in the fact that it was filled with water. The chronicler says it held 3,000 baths (ca. 17,000 gallons) whereas 1 Kings 7:26 says 2,000 (ca. 11,500 gallons). The difference may be that Chronicles is referring to capacity, while Kings is referring to contents. That is, the Sea was kept two-thirds full. As a "sea," it typified the primordial waters of chaos out of which God brought order and the dry land (cf. Gen. 1:2, 9–10). The Lord's victory over the sea is a common theme in the Bible (cf. Exod. 15:8; Ps. 74:13; 78:13; 136:13; etc.) so its presence in the form of this gigantic vessel would be a reminder of his sovereignty, especially in the Exodus deliverance. It also served a "practical" function by providing water with which the priests could wash themselves in preparation for sacrifice (v. 6).

Ten other basins, five on the south side of the Sea and five on the north, served as tubs in which animals brought as burnt offerings were rinsed (v. 6). The author of 1 Kings (7:38) adds the information that each of these basins held 40 baths (ca. 230 gallons) so they were large enough to accommodate the largest animals such as oxen.

The chronicler next lists the articles within the temple beginning with the ten gold lampstands (v. 7). Five of these were on the north side and five on the south in the Holy Place (the meaning of temple here). There were also five tables on each side (apparently for the showbread; cf. v. 19). Elsewhere throughout the temple there were a hundred gold sprinkling bowls (v. 8). The purpose of these is not altogether clear though sprinkling (from. Heb. *zāraq*, "to toss or throw") seems to be in view, perhaps in the sense of application of water or blood in ritual by the use of the fingers or otherwise (cf. Exod. 24:6; Lev. 17:6; Ezek. 36:25).

Moving back outside, the chronicler describes the courtyard

restricted to the priests (the "inner courtyard" of 1 Kings 6:36) and the large court (the outer presumably; cf. 2 Kings 21:5). The doors of both courts were plated with bronze (v. 9). In his usual amplification the author of Kings points out that the walls of the inner court were made of three courses of dressed stone and one of cedar beams (1 Kings 6:36). Evidently then there were two courts surrounding the temple building, the inner one being accessible to the priests alone.

In summary, the account tabulates the furnishings for which Huram was responsible (vv. 11–16). They were the two pillars, the capitals, the chainwork and pomegranates on the capitals, the stands and their basins (not mentioned before but used to support the ten rinsing tubs of v. 6), the Sea with its twelve bulls, the pots (of unknown function, but usually for cooking or washing; cf. 2 Kings 4:38, 39; Jer. 1:13; Ps. 108:9), the shovels (to remove ashes), the meat forks, and other items.

All the preceding were made of bronze or gold. The bronze objects Huram-Abi cast in clay molds in the Jordan Valley between Succoth and Zarethan (vv. 16–17). This site, now well attested archaeologically as a center of the bronze industry, is about 35 miles north of the Dead Sea. So abundant was the production that no effort was made to record it (v. 18).

The gold objects are listed again or, in some cases, for the first time (vv. 19–22). The golden altar, first mentioned here, was the altar of incense (cf. Exod. 37:25–29). The tables are the same as those of verse 8 but here their purpose of holding the bread of the Presence is noted (cf. Exod. 25:23–30). The lampstands, also of gold, stood before the curtain dividing off the Most Holy Place as the narrator here makes clear (v. 20). Other equipment made of gold was the floral work (decoration on the lampstands; cf. Exod. 25:33), the lamps or branches of the lampstands (Exod. 25:37), the tongs (or lampsnuffers; cf. Exod. 25:38), the wick trimmers, sprinkling bowls (v. 8), ladles (or spoons; cf. Exod. 25:29), and censers (in which to burn incense; cf. Lev. 10:1; the Heb. *mahtāh* may also mean "fire-pan"; cf. Exod. 27:3).

Even the doors of both the Holy Place and Most Holy Place were sheathed in gold (v. 22). First Kings 7:50 adds the detail that the very sockets of the doors were gold.

When all was finished, Solomon brought the precious and sacred furnishings into the temple along with silver and gold left over (5:1). These latter he placed in the treasuries of God's temple for safekeeping and future use.

C. The Dedication of the Temple (5:2–7:10)

1. Installation of the Ark (5:2–10)

Following in the footsteps of his father David who had brought the ark of the Lord from Kiriath Jearim into his new tabernacle on Mount Zion (1 Chron. 13:1–5; 15:25–16:3), Solomon convened an assembly of all the leaders of Israel to witness the movement of the ark from that tabernacle to the new temple on Mount Moriah (vv. 2–3). This took place in the seventh month (i.e., Ethanim or Tishri, according to 1 Kings 8:2), coinciding with the Feast of Tabernacles as the chronicler makes clear later (7:8–10; cf. Lev. 23:33–36). This was most appropriate because the Feast of Tabernacles commemorated the wilderness wandering of Israel during which the ark of the Lord was without a permanent resting place (Lev. 23:42–43). Even at Shiloh, Kiriath Jearim, and Mount Zion it was in temporary quarters but now at long last it could rest in the temple Solomon had provided.

First Kings 6:38 notes that the work on the temple took seven years so the date of its dedication and the movement of the ark would have been about 959 B.C. This suggests something of the care that must have gone into the construction and also presupposes sufficient time for Solomon to have established himself as political and religious head of the nation.

When all was ready the Levites, observing proper protocol one may be sure, took up the ark, the other furnishings of the tabernacle, and the very tent itself and brought them all to the temple (vv. 4–5). What they did with all this, particularly the tabernacle, is left to the imagination. Presumably those objects that had no temple function were preserved in some storage area as relics of a past generation.

Preceding the ark, again as David had done, was Solomon the priest-king with his entourage (v. 6; cf. 2 Sam. 6:12–15). As a priest after the order of Melchizedek, he led in the sacrifice of innumerable sheep and oxen (cf. 2 Chron. 5:6 and comments).

The ark was the center of attention for every other furnishing of the temple had been fashioned and put in its place (2 Chron. 3:10–5:1) except this, the very object for which the temple was built. The ark was set within the Most Holy Place under the wings of the cherubim (vv. 7–8), for there was the focus of the presence of the Lord among his people (cf. Exod. 25:21–22). The ark, in fact, represented the throne upon which the Lord sat as sovereign of the earth (cf. Num. 10:35; 1 Sam. 4:4; 2 Sam. 6:2; 2 Kings 19:15; Ezek. 43:7).

Even the poles by which the ark was carried were covered by the cherubim. The narrator makes the helpful observation that the ends of the poles could be seen at certain vantage points from within the Holy Place but not from outside the temple (v. 9). This means that the ark was oriented in a north to south direction for otherwise the poles would protrude through the curtain and not be seen around its ends.

The chronicler (in agreement with 1 Kings 8:9) says there was nothing in the ark but the two stone tablets that Moses had placed there (v. 10; cf. Deut. 10:2–5). The New Testament Book of Hebrews, however, says that the ark also contained Aaron's rod and a pot of manna (Heb. 9:4). The wording here "there was nothing in the ark except the two tablets" might imply that other objects had once been there and no longer were. Moreover, the putting of the manna "in front of the Testimony" (Exod. 16:34) and the rod likewise (Num. 17:10) leads some scholars to suggest that these objects clearly were at least adjacent to the ark and may eventually have been placed within.

2. Praise of the Priests and Levites (5:11–14)

Having set the ark in the Most Holy Place, the priests, without regard for the rotation of service by division, joined the Levitical musicians in a service of praise (vv. 11–14). The Levites represented all three branches of the musical guild (cf. 1 Chron. 15:16–24). They and 120 priests stood on the east side of the great bronze altar, that is, directly in front of the temple's main entrance. Orchestration of cymbals, harps, lyres, and trumpets accompanied in unison the vocal expression of praise to the Lord.

Then, as though in response, a cloud filled the temple, so much so that the priests could no longer carry on the service. The cloud was symbolic of God's glory and attested to his pleasure with the temple and to his having come to invest it with his presence. Elsewhere this manifestation is described as the Shekinah glory (Heb. *šākan*, "to dwell"), the demonstration of God's immanence (cf. Exod. 40:34, 35; Num. 9:15–23; Ezek. 10:3–4).

3. Solomon's Blessing (6:1–11)

As suggested above (5:7–8), the presence of the Lord among his people Israel centered in the ark overshadowed by the cherubim. The ark in turn rested within the Most Holy Place, a chamber that remained always in total darkness. This was not only because of the opaque curtain that shut it off but the dark cloud that continually filled it and spoke of the nearness of the Lord (cf. Exod. 19:9, 16; 24:15–16; 40:34–35; Lev. 16:2, 13; Deut. 4:11; 5:22). In line with that (and not in contrast to it) Solomon says that his temple had become a place in which the Lord would live forever (v. 2).

The king then turned to face the assembly and to bless them. He first praised the Lord who had fulfilled his promise to David regarding a dynastic succession and a temple. Since the day of the Exodus, a day when he manifested his elective grace, God had not chosen either a king or a temple site until he chose David and Mount Moriah (vv. 5–6).

Solomon reminded the people that David had desired to build the temple (1 Chron. 28:2) and though his desire to do so was a noble one, the privilege of bringing it about would fall to his son (1 Chron. 28:5–6). The completed structure attested to the faithfulness of the Lord as did Solomon's kingship (v. 10). And the placing of the ark within the temple certified that the covenant the Lord had made with his people was still intact (v. 11).

4. Solomon's Prayer (6:12–42)

All this time Solomon had been standing on a bronze platform five cubits (7 1/2 feet) square and three cubits (4 1/2 feet) high situated in the courtyard before the great bronze altar (vv. 12–13). He now knelt down, spreading his hands toward heaven, and offered a prayer of dedication and supplication.

He first praised the incomparable God of Israel who had faithfully kept his covenant promises (literally, "the covenant and the *ḥesed*" or "the commitment to covenant"). The standing temple bore witness to that fact (vv. 14–15). On the basis of his past faithfulness, Solomon entreated the Lord to preserve the dynasty of David forever as his successors walked in covenant obedience (vv. 16–17).

Then, in one of the most profound theological confessions in all of Scripture, Solomon distinguished between God's presence in the temple as represented by the ark and the cloud of glory on the one hand and his transcendent habitation of the universe on the other. Indeed, Solomon said, even the universe cannot contain the Lord (v. 18)!

Nevertheless, God heard human prayer and did so in particular and peculiar ways in connection with the temple. It was there that he promised to place his name (that is, to locate his presence; cf. 1 Chron. 13:6). Thereafter, his people would pray to him by addressing themselves toward the temple (cf. Dan. 6:10) and as they did so in repentant faith he would hear from heaven and would forgive their sins (vv. 20–21).

The temple served also as a place of adjudication between men (vv. 22–23). When a man came there to swear to his innocence in a legal matter (cf. Exod. 22:8–11; Deut. 17:8–9), then, prayed Solomon, might the Lord either confirm his innocence or expose his guilt.

If the people of Israel suffered military defeat because of their disobedience but then sought the Lord's forgiveness at the temple through suitable supplication, would that God might hear and answer their prayer and restore them to their land and homes (vv. 24–25).

Continuing, Solomon pleaded that in the event of drought occasioned by the sin of the people they might find instruction

and forgiveness as they looked to the Lord at the temple and that
God might send the rains again upon the thirsty land (vv. 26–
27). Likewise, when natural disasters of whatever kind came
and the people sought the Lord in his temple, might he hear
from his actual dwelling place in heaven and offer his forgiveness according to the sin and the response of each and every
individual so that they might profit from it and learn to live
according to the ways of the Lord (vv. 28–31).

Even the foreigner ought to have access to the Lord by
means of the temple, Solomon implored, for in doing so he
could attest to the universality of the sovereignty and awesomeness of Israel's God. He could know and would confess
that the temple in Jerusalem marked the special presence of the
Lord in the earth (vv. 32–33).

In the event of war, Solomon prayed, might the Lord give
victory to his people as they looked to him at the temple (vv.
34–35). But if the worst came and the people should be carried
off as exiles to a distant land—a very real possibility given their
penchant for sin—would that God might hear their repentant
cry directed to the Lord in his holy temple. From heaven might
he respond with forgiveness and uphold their cause (vv. 36–39;
cf. Lev. 26:40–42; Neh. 9:2).

Finally, Solomon once more urged the Lord to be sensitive
to prayer offered in connection with the temple (v. 40) and
concluded his petition with a hymnic selection paraphrased
from Psalm 132:8–10. He invited the Lord to come to his resting
place (the temple) with the ark that spoke of his presence
(v. 41a). He prayed that the priests might continue to be clothed
in the Lord's salvation and that the people (the saints) might
enjoy his goodness (v. 41b). Then he prayed for himself,
describing himself as the "anointed one" (Heb. *māšîaḥ*, "messiah"), an epithet entirely appropriate in light of the Lord's
covenant promises to David (cf. 1 Sam. 2:10; Ps. 2:2; 18:50;
89:39, 51; 132:17).

5. Solomon's Sacrifices (7:1–10)

The Lord showed his favorable attention to Solomon's
prayer by sending down fire from heaven that consumed the
sacrifices on the great bronze altar (v. 1). Thus he often did to

remove any question in people's minds that he was pleased and that he would act in response to their prayer (1 Kings 18:38–39; Judg. 6:19–21). Further confirmation was in the appearance of God's glory, an appearance so overwhelming in its intensity and awesomeness that the priests could not enter the temple and the people could only fall prostrate in wonder and praise proclaiming God's goodness and his love (Heb. *ḥesed*, "covenant loyalty").

Solomon then offered a massive sacrifice of 22,000 cattle and 120,000 sheep and goats as a tangible act of dedication (vv. 4–5). With sound of instruments the Levites joined the priests in lifting up praises to the Lord, once again underlining the Lord's *ḥesed*, his commitment to his covenant promises (v. 6). So numerous were the sacrifices, Solomon consecrated the entire forecourt of the temple and made it in its entirety a vast altar upon which he could offer the burnt offerings and fellowship (or peace) offerings (v. 7; cf. 1 Chron. 16:1–3).

Following this glorious day of dedication, Solomon extended the festivities for seven more days making a total, it seems, of fifteen days. This is based on the chronicler's statement that the dedication itself had taken seven days (commencing with the assembly of 2 Chron. 5:2, which occurred in the seventh month; v. 3). The assembly of the eighth day (v. 9) was the climax of the Feast of Tabernacles, which began on the fifteenth day of the seventh month and extended through the twenty-second (Lev. 23:34–36). The eighth day, then, refers to the final convocation of the Feast of Tabernacles on the twenty-second day of the month. This implies that the dedication ceremony of 2 Chronicles 5:2 commenced on the eighth day of that month. Since the Day of Atonement (Yom Kippur) fell on the tenth day of the seventh month (Lev. 23:27), it must have occupied an important part of the ceremony of temple dedication, probably coinciding with the procession and installation of the ark (2 Chron. 5:2–14).

The multitudes of Israel—from Lebo Hamath (cf. 1 Chron. 13:5) in the North to the Wadi of Egypt (the Wadi el-Arish, just south of Gaza) in the South—kept the festival of the eighth day of the Feast of Tabernacles and then returned to their homes the next day, the twenty-third of the month (v. 10). Their hearts were filled with gratitude to God for his goodness to them and to their king.

D. The Conditions of Covenant Blessing (7:11–22)

About eight years after completing the temple (cf. 1 Kings 6:37–7:1; 2 Chron. 5:2 and comments), Solomon had completed the construction of his own palace bringing him to the midpoint of his forty-year reign (2 Chron. 8:1). It was appropriate that the Lord should visit with him again at that point to remind him that the success he had achieved was a beneficence of God's grace and that its continuation could be possible only as Solomon and the people remained in covenant fellowship with him.

The Lord first reminded Solomon of the suitability of the temple as the focus of his accessibility on the earth. It was the place to which his people must come for sacrifice (v. 12).

Then, in a brief recapitulation of the conditions that would call down the judgment of the Lord upon his people (cf. 6:18–42), he outlined the means by which their sin could be forgiven and their land healed: They must confess, repent, and return to him (vv. 13–14). This must be in connection with the temple for it was there that the Lord had chosen to place his Name, that is, to manifest his presence (v. 16).

Solomon himself could expect the blessing of God by the establishment and perpetuation of his dynasty as he had promised David (v. 17; cf. 2 Sam. 7:13, 25), but this presupposed single-minded devotion to the Lord and obedience of the covenant stipulations (cf. 1 Chron. 22:12–13). Disobedience, particularly in terms of idolatry, would result in deportation of the people and rejection of the temple (vv. 19–20). Idolatry was so opprobrious because it epitomized covenant disloyalty, the repudiation of the Lord's sovereignty, and the acceptance of another god (cf. Deut. 4:15–24). It was for covenant violation that Solomon suffered the judgment of the Lord (cf. 1 Kings 11:9–13) and Israel and Judah eventually went into Assyrian (2 Kings 17:7–18) and Babylonian Exile (Jer. 32:26–35).

Evidence of God's displeasure with his people would be most apparent in the destruction of the glorious temple of Solomon (vv. 20–22). This indeed took place (2 Chron. 36:17–21) and for the reasons and with the results that the Lord revealed to Solomon (Lam. 1:1–11). Its very ruins would testify to the unfaithfulness of God's people and to the certainty and righteousness of his judgment. Yet, as Solomon himself had previously avowed, that judgment could be overturned as the nation repented (6:36–39; 7:14), and the temple could and must be rebuilt in conformity with God's promise of its unending existence (6:1–2).

E. Solomon's Accomplishments (8:1–9:31)

1. Political Achievements (8:1–11)

Halfway through his reign, his great building projects having been brought to a successful conclusion, Solomon began to address matters of a broader, more distant concern. Though the chronicler omits the narrative, 1 Kings 9:10–14 relates the story that Solomon had ceded certain Galilean cities over to Hiram in exchange for timber and gold. Hiram later discovered that the cities were not up to his expectations and, in fact, he called them Cabul (Heb. for "as good as nothing"). It is likely that the statement here ("Solomon rebuilt the villages that Hiram had given him") refers to the return of these very towns that Solomon, reluctantly no doubt, had to take back. In any event, Solomon sent Israelite settlers to occupy these places (v. 2).

He also undertook military campaigns to the far North. He captured Hamath Zobah, an Aramean city that David before him had conquered (v. 3; cf. 1 Chron. 18:3, 9–10). He even went so far as to fortify Tadmor (later, Palmyra), a desert oasis more than 150 miles northeast of Damascus. Occupation of such strategic trading centers gave Solomon the kind of control of commercial activity between Egypt on the one hand and Anatolia and Mesopotamia on the other hand that would enable him to prosper as he did (cf. 9:13–14).

Within Israel's borders, Solomon rebuilt Upper Beth-Horon (10 miles northwest of Jerusalem), Lower Beth-Horon (3 miles farther west), and Baalath (ca. 20 miles west of Jerusalem). These all lay on important trade routes in valleys crossing the land from east to west. In addition, he strengthened the walls and gates of many other cities where he stored provisions and quartered his horses and chariots (v. 6).

The indigenous, non-Israelite peoples of the land, such as Hittites, Amorites, Perizzites (an Amorite people of the hill country of Judah; Josh. 11:3; 12:8; 17:15; 24:11), Hivites (probably the same as the Indo-Aryan Hurrians), and Jebusites (cf. 1 Chron. 20:18) Solomon reduced to slave labor. These had not been driven from Canaan at the time of the Israelite conquest and, in fact, their bondage as servants had long been predicted (Josh. 16:10; cf. 9:27).

The Israelites were exempt from such demeaning labor but were enlisted in the armies and as supervisors over civil works projects (vv. 9–10).

One of Solomon's major international relationships was with the Pharaoh of Egypt (probably Siamun of Dynasty 21) whose daughter he had taken as wife early in his reign (cf. 1 Kings 3:1). He settled her first in the City of David (Zion) until he could build his own palace and suitable facilities for her as well. The reason Solomon was eager to move her, the chronicler says, is because she as a pagan would defile the palace of David, which itself had been so closely identified with the ark of the Lord (v. 11). The marriage, however, had significance beyond this because it suggests that Solomon enjoyed parity with the great rulers of the world.

2. Religious Achievements (8:12–16)

In religious affairs Solomon was careful to attend to the requirements of public worship though, as Kings shows in detail, he made fatal compromises with idolatry in his personal life that inevitably translated into a problem of national dimensions (1 Kings 11:1–8). Despite this, the chronicler's view that he offered the prescribed burnt offerings on the stated occasions cannot be denied. These included the morning and evening offerings of the lamb (Exod. 29:38–42), the Sabbath observance (Lev. 23:3), the New Moon festivals (Num. 10:10), and the thrice-annual convocations—the Feast of Unleavened Bread (Lev. 23:4–14), the Feast of Weeks (Lev. 23:15–21), and the Feast of Tabernacles (Lev. 23:33–36).

Furthermore, he continued the structure of cultic personnel

established by his father by appointing priests, Levites, gate-keepers, and others as vacancies occurred or other needs required (v. 14). Scrupulously these officials carried out the wishes of the king (v. 15) for they recognized him as the vice-regent of the Lord himself, the one who in a practical sense was in charge of religious as well as political affairs.

Last, but most important, Solomon had undertaken and completed the building of the temple (v. 16). By any measurement this was his most impressive accomplishment, one that laid the foundation for all of Israel's subsequent religious life and practice.

3. Economic Achievements (8:17–9:28)

At some point in their relationship Solomon and Hiram entered into a joint maritime industry in which the Phoenicians supplied ships and officers and the Israelites seamen to ply the trade routes from Ezion Geber and Elath to distant lands, such as Ophir (8:17–18). Ezion Geber and Elath were ports on the eastern arm of the Red Sea, now known as the Gulf of Aqaba or the Gulf of Elath (cf. Num. 33:35; Deut. 2:8). The area alternately lay within the domination of Edom or Israel. Ophir was a source of many precious commodities, especially gold (cf. 1 Chron. 29:4). Apparently on one voyage alone the cargo amounted to 450 talents (17 tons) of gold. Such enterprises help to explain the immense wealth of Solomon's kingdom (cf. 9:13).

Evidence of Solomon's international stature may be seen in the account of the visit of the queen of Sheba to Jerusalem (9:1–12). She had heard of his great wisdom and so she came with a caravan of spices, gold, and precious stones to engage him in conversation. Her interest and seriousness may be gauged by the fact that she came more than 1,200 miles to see him.

Sheba (or Saba; cf. Gen. 10:7, 28; 25:3) was a region in South Arabia fabled for its abundant resources in gold (Ps. 72:15) and incense (Jer. 6:20; Isa. 60:6; Ezek. 27:22). The fact that the queen of Sheba could give Solomon 120 talents (ca. 4 1/2 tons) of gold, besides spices and precious stones, as a gesture of her goodwill (v. 9) attests to the wealth of her land.

But as rich as she was, she was impressed beyond belief by what she saw and heard in Jerusalem. She was overwhelmed by the sagacity of her host and by the splendor of his court and kingdom (vv. 2–4). She could only remark that the reality of what she saw far outweighed her anticipation of it (vv. 5–6). With unusual theological insight she concluded that the officials who served Solomon must be happy indeed to be a part of such a kingdom. How worthy of praise, she exclaimed, is the God who placed Solomon as king over his people Israel and who established justice and righteousness through him (vv. 7–8).

The gifts she left were only part of the imports that enriched Israel. As already noted, the sailors of Hiram and Solomon had acquired gold from Ophir (v. 10; cf. 9:18). They also brought algum-wood (or almug-wood; cf. 1 Kings 10:11) to make stairways for the temple and palace, and harps and lyres for the musicians (v. 11). So rich was Solomon he gave to the queen of Sheba more than she had brought to him (v. 12). Thus, it was plain for the whole world to see that the God of Israel had prospered his people and their king more than any other nation on the earth.

As a kind of inventory list illustrative of the economic prosperity of Solomon's court and kingdom, the chronicler draws attention to various and sundry data (vv. 13–21). The king's income through taxation alone was 666 talents (about 25 tons) per year. In addition were the profits gained through international trade and tribute (vv. 13–14). Reference to "the kings of Arabia" and "the governors of the land" suggests that the flow to the royal coffers came from outside as well as inside Israel. Since there was no difference between the king's holdings and those of the state, what is in view here is the financial resources of the nation as a whole.

With this vast amount of gold, the artisans of the king made 200 large shields of 600 bekas (about 7 1/2 pounds) each and 300 small shields of 300 bekas (about 3 3/4 pounds) each. These were housed in a public building called the Palace of the Forest of Lebanon, so named because it was constructed largely of cedar timbers from Lebanon (cf. 1 Kings 7:2–6).

Other gold was used to plate his royal throne whose beauty was further enhanced by ivory inlay (v. 17). The throne had six steps, a gold footstool, and armrests on each side guarded by a lion figurine. Twelve other such statues stood on the steps of the throne, one on either end of each step (vv. 18–19).

All the king's goblets were also of gold as were the household articles in the Palace of the Forest of Lebanon (v. 20). With perhaps some hyperbole, the narrator says that silver was not used at all because in Solomon's day it had so little relative value. In the spirit of collecting the rare and precious, Solomon sent out ships of Tarshish (merchant ships, so-called because they were capable of traveling great distances; cf. Jonah 1:3). Once every three years these fleets went forth, commanded by Phoenician mariners (cf. 8:18). On their return they came loaded with such luxuries as gold, silver, and ivory and with objects of curiosity including apes and baboons (v. 21; so NIV; other versions translate Heb. *tūkkîyîm* as "peacocks").

All the preceding was just to make the point that Solomon excelled all other kings in riches and wisdom (v. 22). Like the queen of Sheba, they came to hear his words of wisdom and to see with their own eyes the splendor of his court. And as was typical and expected they profferred their expressions of tribute in such lavish gifts as silver, gold, robes, weapons, spices, horses, and mules (vv. 23–24).

The horses and mules, the former being necessary accoutrements of a powerful military force, required maintenance so Solomon had 4,000 (the 40,000 of 1 Kings 4:26 is a scribal slip) stalls for his 12,000 horses and their chariots. These were located in "chariot cities" (cf. 8:6) strategically placed throughout the land and in Jerusalem as well (v. 25). With these in support of his armies, he ruled all the region from "the River" (the Euphrates) to (but not including) Philistia as far as the border of Egypt (v. 26). This domination explains how it was that the chronicler (again hyperbolically) could attribute to Solomon such wealth that silver was as common as mere pebbles and cedar as plentiful as sycamore-fig trees (v. 27; cf. 1:15–17). It explains also why Solomon enjoyed such status among the great kings of the earth (such as the king of Egypt) that they welcomed his commercial enterprises (v. 28).

4. A Historical Summation (9:29–31)

As a conclusion to the narrative of Solomon, the historian cites other documents where further information might be found. These are the records of Nathan the prophet (cf. 1 Chron. 29:29), Ahijah the Shilonite (cf. 1 Kings 11:29; 12:15; 14:2), and Iddo the seer (cf. 2 Chron. 12:15; 13:22), the last of whom evidently composed an account concerning Jeroboam son of Nebat (cf. 1 Kings 11:26).

In all, Solomon reigned forty years (971–931 B.C.). Upon his death he was buried in the City of David (that is, Mount Zion; cf. 1 Kings 2:10), resting with his fathers, and was succeeded by his son Rehoboam (vv. 30–31).

For Futher Study

1. Attempt to sketch the temple and its surroundings on the basis of the biblical descriptions. Read an article on the temple of Solomon in a Bible dictionary or encyclopedia.

2. List the principal furnishings and features of the temple, compare them to those of the Mosaic Tabernacle, and try to determine the symbolism of each.

3. Prepare an outline of Solomon's prayer of dedication of the temple (2 Chron. 6:12–42). Note the principal elements of the prayer and trace the major theological themes and motifs.

4. Account for the chronicler's relative inattention to the polygamy and idolatry of Solomon that the author of Kings (1 Kings 11) emphasizes as the reasons for his fall from favor.

Chapter 5

The Dynasty of David: Rehoboam to Uzziah
(2 Chronicles 10:1–25:28)

A. The Reign of Rehoboam (10:1–12:16)

1. The Division of the Kingdom (10:1–11:4)

Rehoboam was a son of Solomon by his wife Naamah the Ammonite (2 Chron. 12:13). The fact that he was forty-one when he began to reign and that Solomon reigned for forty years (12:13; cf. 9:30) suggests that Rehoboam was born during Solomon's co-regency with David and may have been the child of a union undertaken for purposes of amicable relationships between Israel and Ammon in David's last years (cf. 1 Kings 11:1).

In any case Rehoboam, evidently Solomon's eldest son, succeeded him as king. So tenuous was the transition, however, that Rehoboam went to Shechem for the coronation ceremony rather than Jerusalem where it would be expected (v. 1). Shechem was, of course, a place of ancient covenant tradition (cf. Gen. 12:6–7; 35:4; Josh. 24:1–28), but for Rehoboam to resort there on this occasion was to concede that the longstanding rift between Judah and the northern tribes was still in effect and that Solomon's death was all that was needed to destroy the union completely. To preclude this, Rehoboam met the representatives of the North in their own place and essentially on their own terms.

Meanwhile, Jeroboam son of Nebat, who had just returned from Egyptian exile, headed up the Israelite delegation that met with Rehoboam. Jeroboam had served as a supervisor of

Solomon's work gangs in the region of Ephraim (1 Kings 11:26–28), and one day he was approached by the prophet Ahijah who told him he would someday rule over the ten northern tribes (1 Kings 11:31–32). When Solomon heard about this, he tried to kill Jeroboam, but Jeroboam fled to Egypt where he remained until Solomon died.

The demand Jeroboam made was that the heavy yoke of work and taxes (cf. 1 Kings 4:7; 9:15; 1 Sam. 8:11–18) that Solomon had placed on the people be made lighter. After a three-day delay in the negotiations during which Rehoboam consulted with his advisers, he returned to the conclave with his response. His elders who had served Solomon advised him to go along with the demands of the people and relieve their burdens (v. 7). Rehoboam rejected this counsel, however, and proceeded to announce the opinion of his young peers. Rather than reduce the onerous weight of bondage to the state Rehoboam said he was going to increase it (vv. 13–14).

Using metaphorical language, Rehoboam harshly proclaimed that the severity of his rule compared to that of his father would be the same as the difference between a mere whip and a scorpion (v. 14). A scorpion was likely a whip containing sharp pieces of metal that lacerated the flesh when it was employed in beating.

The result was predictable, for Rehoboam's obdurateness was itself a part of the purpose of God for his people. Ahijah the prophet had previously informed Jeroboam that he would lead a successful rebellion against David's house because of Solomon's apostasy (1 Kings 11:33). Rehoboam would retain only the tribe of Judah, David's own tribe, while Jeroboam would become the first king of Israel, the name thenceforth applied to the northern tribes.

The "declaration of independence" (v. 16) asked the question "what share do we have in David?" This same sentiment had actually been expressed in David's own lifetime (2 Sam. 20:1) but its roots were much earlier. From the time of David's anointing and later alienation from Saul (cf. 1 Sam. 16:12–14; 22:1–2) a rift had developed between his followers and those of Saul. This rift was clearly along tribal lines with David's support coming primarily from his own tribe of Judah and Saul's from the remainder of the nation. The separation between Rehoboam and Jeroboam was just the natural and inevitable result of a historical process of long duration.

Rehoboam did not give up without a struggle nor was the cleavage absolute. There were Israelites living in Judah who submitted themselves to Rehoboam's rule (v. 17), and Rehoboam also made overtures of a peaceful nature to effect a reunification. He sent Hadoram (or Adoniram; cf. 1 Kings 4:6), director of his conscripted labor and thus counterpart to Jeroboam, to seek reconciliation but the mobs of Israel stoned him to death (v. 18). Sensing the futility and danger of further rapprochement, Rehoboam returned to Jerusalem leaving the nation divided. This condition, the chronicler says, existed to his very day, that is, till after the Exile (ca. 450 B.C.).

Rebuffed for his peaceful approach, Rehoboam decided to take military measures (11:1–4). He raised a mighty host of 180,000 men to launch an attack on Israel and bring the rebels back under his control. The historian notes here that these men came not only from Judah but from Benjamin as well (v. 1). How and when Benjamin joined the kingdom of Judah is not clear for Ahijah had prophesied that the tribe of Judah alone would be loyal to Rehoboam at the time of the schism (1 Kings 11:32). Apparently (and ironically since Benjamin was the tribe of Saul), Benjamin affiliated with Judah shortly after the break and probably because of its close geographic proximity to both Judah and Jerusalem. Interestingly enough, moreover, it was the tribe of Benjamin that had most warmly welcomed David back to Jerusalem after his return from exile in the coup of Absalom (2 Sam. 19:16–20; cf. 40–43).

Rehoboam's military move never got underway, for Shemaiah, a prophet of God, reminded the king once more that the division of the kingdom was an act of God. Obediently but no doubt with great reluctance, Rehoboam abandoned his offensive strategy and set about to establish defensive positions that would at least guarantee his own freedom from Israelite threats.

2. Rehoboam's Rule and Family (11:5–23)

In light of the hostility engendered by the rupture of the kingdom, Rehoboam proceeded to develop a structure of

defense organized around some fifteen cities scattered throughout Judah and Benjamin (vv. 5–12). These extended from
Aijalon in the North to Ziph in the South and from Tekoa in the
East to Gath in the West. Each of these was heavily fortified and
supplied with garrisons of troops and provisions of weapons and
foods in the event of siege. Again the chronicler emphasizes that
both Judah and Benjamin belonged to Rehoboam.

He also points out that the religious establishment admit-
tedly remained loyal to the Davidic crown, though partly at least
because Jeroboam rejected the authorized priesthood and
Levites in favor of his own appointees (vv. 13–15; cf. 1 Kings
12:25–33). Abandoning lands and goods, the Levites moved
south encouraging many of the laity to do likewise from all over
the northern kingdom (v. 16). The reference to three years
(v. 17) suggests that the movement of the people to Judah was
not in the form of a migration but was associated with the annual
festivals in Jerusalem to which the devout of all Israel were
invited (Deut. 12:5–7). It was the continuance of this very
practice that convinced Jeroboam that he needed to set up his
own rival cult in the North to preclude the regular pilgrimages
of his people to Jerusalem (1 Kings 12:27). Thus, he removed
the legitimate priests and Levites from their positions and
installed his own (v. 15). It took three years to accomplish this, a
time in which Rehoboam enjoyed the support of the faithful of
the northern kingdom.

Turning to the matter of Rehoboam's family, the chronicler
singles out two wives (out of 18 plus 60 concubines, v. 21) for
special mention. The first was Mahalath, a granddaughter of
David through one line and of Jesse through another (v. 18).
Jerimoth son of David is not elsewhere mentioned and he may
be a grandson. Eliab was Jesse's eldest son (1 Sam. 16:6) but his
daughter Abihail appears nowhere else in the record. The real
purpose of the chronicler in any case is not to make precise
identifications but to establish Rehoboam's solid connections to
the Davidic dynasty even by marriage, something the author of
Kings fails to do.

The second wife named, Maacah, is of more importance
because she was the mother of Abijah, the next king of Judah
(vv. 20, 22). Her name appears elsewhere as Micaiah the

daughter of Uriel (13:2) whereas here she is the daughter of Absalom (or Abishalom in 1 Kings 15:10). Since Absalom, son of David, apparently left no male offspring (cf. 2 Sam. 14:27; 18:18), the Absalom here cannot be he. Furthermore, Micaiah (or Maacah) was of a family from Gibeah, Saul's hometown (2 Chron. 13:2), so it is likely she was a Benjamite. Such a marriage arrangement would work well to solidify the Judah-Benjamin alliance. As to Maacah's father, if he was Absalom his father may have been Uriel. The converse is also a possibility, of course.

Because Rehoboam loved Maacah more than all his other wives, he appointed her son Abijah (or Abijam; cf. 1 Kings 15:1) to be his royal successor, evidently elevating him to a position of vice-regent (v. 22). The other sons, of whom there were twenty-seven in addition to Abijah (v. 21), he did not neglect, however, for he appointed them as rulers over the fortified cities and other important centers throughout the land. He provided for them handsomely and enhanced their prestige by acquiring many wives for each one (v. 23).

3. God's Judgment and the Summation of Rehoboam's Reign (12:1–16)

Like his father before him, Rehoboam responded to the blessing and prosperity of the Lord by leading his people into covenant disloyalty (v. 1). As punishment the Egyptian king Shishak (also Sheshonq or Shoshenq in Egyptian texts), founder of the twenty-second dynasty, invaded Egypt with 1,200 chariots, 60,000 cavalry, and countless infantry made up of Libyans, Sukkites (perhaps from the deserts of western Libya), and Cushites (or Ethiopians). The result was the capture of many of Judah's fortified cities (cf. 11:5–10) and threat to Jerusalem itself (vv. 1–4).

This campaign the historian dates in the fifth year of Rehoboam (v. 2) or 926 B.C. Shishak, whose dates are about 935–914 B.C., was the king who had provided haven to Jeroboam when Jeroboam fled to Egypt from Solomon (cf. 1 Kings 11:40). Perhaps his attack on Judah was at least partly for the purpose of weakening Judah for the benefit of Jeroboam and Israel. The record of his conquest inscribed on the temple walls at Karnak in Egypt reveals, however, that he invaded even Israel itself. His successes in Judah no doubt made him thirsty for further exploits.

If there was any doubt as to the theological meaning of this state of affairs, Shemaiah the prophet (cf. 11:2) soon shed some light. Addressing the frightened leadership of Jerusalem, he put his finger on the cause of their predicament—they had abandoned the Lord so he had abandoned them (v. 5). In deep and genuine repentance, the king and his officials confessed the justice of God's dealings with them. To this the Lord responded with a message of forgiveness and deliverance from destruction (vv. 6–7). Judah would, however, be subservient to Egypt for a time until they could learn once more how blessed by comparison was the sovereignty of the Lord (v. 8).

Evidence of the vassalship was the payment to Shishak of all valuables of both the temple and the royal palace (v. 9). The treasuries were so depleted that objects of gold had to be replaced by objects of bronze. Fearful lest even the bronze shields that replaced the older ones of gold should be stolen, Rehoboam commanded that they be locked up in the guardroom when they were not in use (vv. 10–11). God's judgment would have been even more severe had not the king repented. Indeed, the chronicler says, "there was some good in Judah" (v. 12).

By way of summarizing Rehoboam's reign, the historian reaffirms his overall strength and stability. He had suffered reverses such as the Egyptian invasion to be sure, but he did reign for seventeen years (931–914 B.C. inclusive) and managed to do so from Jerusalem, the city chosen by the Lord as his own dwelling-place (v. 13). The fact that his mother was an Ammonite, however, cannot be dissociated from the assessment that Rehoboam was an evil man who did not set his heart on the Lord (v. 14). The paganism of the parent clearly was a negative influence on the son.

Characteristically, the chronicler mentions that other information relative to Rehoboam's reign can be found in the records of Shemaiah the prophet (cf. v. 5) and Iddo the seer (cf. 9:29), records that he describes as genealogies (v. 15). Overriding everything else was the incessant warfare between Israel and

Judah during this period, the narratives of which are, however, strangely missing in both Kings and Chronicles.

Finally, Rehoboam died and like his father Solomon was buried in the royal tombs in the City of David (cf. 9:31). His son and co-regent Abijah then sat on his throne.

B. The Reign of Abijah (13:1–14:1)

Abijah began his three-year reign (914–911 B.C.) in the eighteenth year of Jeroboam of Israel. This was also the seventeenth of Rehoboam since he reigned for that many years in all (12:13). The reason that Abijah's first year was the eighteenth of Jeroboam and only the seventeenth of Rehoboam though both began to reign at the same time is that Israel used a system of chronology that regarded any part of a year as a whole year while Judah counted only full years. Thus, three years of Abijah would correctly be 914–911. (For comments on his mother see 11:20.)

The only event of Abijah's short reign that receives any attention is his war with Jeroboam (v. 2). What prompted this engagement is unknown but it was on a massive scale as the 400,000 men of Judah and 800,000 of Israel attests. Standing on Mount Zemaraim, not far southwest of Bethel in Ephraim (cf. Josh. 18:22), Abijah addressed the Israelites who lay in battle formation before him. He reminded them that the true covenant kingship belonged to the dynasty of David in Judah and that it was forever as the term "covenant of salt" made clear (v. 5; cf. Lev. 2:13; Num. 18:19). The kingship of Jeroboam was a usurpation, he said, a rump movement of scoundrels who took advantage of Rehoboam's youth and weakness (vv. 6–7).

Abijah conceded that Israel came with an enormous host (v. 8), but the religious underpinnings of the nation were idolatrous and completely without legal sanction (v. 9). The implication is that such an illegitimate system as Israel represented was hardly to be considered a threat to God's people.

Judah, on the other hand, worshiped the Lord and had remained loyal to him (but cf. 1 Kings 15:3). Her priests and Levites could trace their descent to Aaron and Levi, they observed the ritual in a prescribed manner, and otherwise observed the requirements of the Law (vv. 10–11). As a result,

God was with Judah and as a mighty warrior he would lead his
hosts in holy war (cf. Num. 10:8–9). It would be foolhardy for
Israel to resist him, Abijah concluded (v. 12).

But Jeroboam took no heed and sent a part of his army to the
rear of Judah's troops. When they saw they were surrounded,
they cried out to the Lord, blew the trumpets, and shouted, all in
line with the procedures of holy war (cf. Josh. 6:15–21).
Emphatically the historian stresses that "God routed Jeroboam"
(v. 15) and "God delivered them into their hands" (v. 16). In
all, the Israelites suffered 500,000 casualties for the Lord was
with Judah (v. 17).

The spoils of victory included the capture of Bethel, the
southern center of Jeroboam's illicit cult (cf. 1 Kings 12:29),
Jeshanah (perhaps el-Burj, 6 miles north of Bethel), and Ephron,
4 miles northeast of Bethel (v. 19). Jeroboam never recovered
his power and influence and died before long (in 910 B.C.).
Abijah, however, grew in strength as the accumulation of
fourteen wives, twenty-two sons, and sixteen daughters testifies.
The political and military status of an ancient Near Eastern king
was frequently measured in terms of the size of his harem and
the number of his children.

Further information on the deeds and sayings of Abijah may
be found, the chronicler says, in the records of Iddo the prophet
(v. 22; cf. 9:29). The last notation he himself makes is that
Abijah died, he was buried with his ancestors in the City of
David (cf. 9:31; 12:16), and he was succeeded by his son Asa.
This introduced a period of ten years of peace (911–901 B.C.) in
Judah (14:1).

C. The Reign of Asa (14:2–16:14).

1. Asa's Political and Military Success (14:2–15)

Asa, the third king of Judah, reigned for forty-one years
(911–870 B.C.; cf. 16:13). Since his first ten years were years of
peace (cf. 14:1), there is no reference to his dealings with
Jeroboam with whom he was contemporary for about one year
(Jeroboam's dates are 931–910 B.C.; cf. 1 Kings 14:20). Also, the
chronicler arranged his history around persons and events in
Judah (contrary to the account in Kings, which focuses mainly

on Israel) and mentioned Israel's kings only if and when they were relevant to Judah. Thus, Jeroboam and even his son Nadab, who reigned for two years over Israel (910–909 B.C.; cf. 1 Kings 15:25), are bypassed in Chronicles during Asa's reign.

The account concerning Asa begins with a statement of commendation: He did "what was good and right in the eyes of the LORD His God" (v. 2). This manifested itself in the removal of such pagan elements as altars, high places (the sites of heathen worship), sacred stones (Heb. *maṣṣēbôt,* "pillars"), and Asherah poles (v. 3). The latter two objects were related to the Canaanite fertility cults and originally at least connoted the most grossly sensual and immoral significance. They probably had been introduced or at least tolerated by Solomon himself (cf. 1 Kings 11:5–8).

On the positive side, Asa encouraged his people to seek the Lord and to keep all the covenant requirements (v. 4). He also rebuilt the fortified cities, which apparently had come back under Judah's control because of the devotion of the king to the Lord (vv. 5–7). Rehoboam had first established them throughout the countryside (cf. 2 Chron. 11:5–12), but Shishak had come and taken them (12:4). Now with the decline of Egypt and resurgence of Judah under Asa, the original territories were reclaimed.

His ten years of respite from war (14:1) gave Asa opportunity to build up his military strength (v. 8). He mustered 300,000 men from Judah and 280,000 from Benjamin, all brave and well-equipped. Whether this was done because Asa knew of Egypt's recovery or not, it was well timed because Egypt once more invaded Judah, this time under the command of Zerah the Cushite (or Ethiopian).

Zerah was evidently a mercenary who hired out his vast army (Heb. says "a thousand thousand" men, v. 9) and 300 chariots to Egypt whose king by then was Osorkon I (914–874 B.C.), next in line after Shishak. Before the Cushites could arrive in Judah proper, Asa met them near Mareshah, one of his fortified cities (11:8) about 25 miles southwest of Jerusalem (vv. 9–10). In utter dependence on God, Asa cried out to him to defend them and to maintain his own integrity (v. 11).

The Lord intervened and Judah achieved a decisive victory

over the Cushites, pursuing them as far as Gerar, which lay more than 20 miles farther to the southwest, perhaps within Egyptian territorial claims. Cushites fell everywhere and Gerar and its surrounding towns yielded their spoil to Asa's victorious armies (vv. 12–14). Even the nomadic herdsmen fell victim, surrendering their sheep, goats, and camels to the Judeans who then returned triumphantly to Jerusalem (v. 15).

2. Asa's Religious Successes (15:1–19)

Not too long after Asa's victory over Zerah (specifically in his fifteenth year or 896 B.C.; cf. v. 10), Azariah the son of Oded, a prophet of the Lord mentioned only here, came to the king with the affirming word that the Lord was with him and his kingdom. That could continue, he said, as long as the people were true to the Lord and kept on seeking him (vv. 1–2). They must not repeat the mistakes of their fathers who were without God and priest and law (v. 3). This must refer to the time of the judges, a period of Israel's history marked by political and religious anarchy (cf. Judg. 17:6; 18:1; 19:1; 21:25).

As a result of such defection from the Lord, there was a breakdown of law and order, war between nations (probably tribes; cf. Judg. 20) and cities, and all kinds of distress (vv. 5–6). When their fathers turned to the Lord, however, he turned to them and forgave them (cf. Judg. 2:11–23). He would likewise be with Asa and his generation if they persisted in their pursuit of godliness (vv. 4, 7).

Encouraged by these words, Asa redoubled his efforts to rid the land of every vestige of idolatry. He purged the idols not only from Judah and Benjamin but even from the towns in Ephraim he had captured (probably actually done by Abijah; cf. 13:19). He also repaired the great bronze altar of the temple, which had either suffered damage or had been allowed to deteriorate (v. 8).

Next Asa convened a great assembly consisting of Judeans, Benjamites, and even Israelites from Ephraim and Manasseh who fled to Judah from their home districts when they saw how God was blessing Asa and his kingdom (v. 9). The convocation, dated by the chronicler in the third month of Asa's fifteenth year (896 B.C.), featured a sacrifice of 700 cattle and 7,000 sheep and goats plundered, most likely, from the Cushites (v. 11; cf. 14:15). This was followed by a service of covenant commitment in which the people pledged to seek the Lord wholeheartedly and to purge from among them any who refused to do so (vv. 12–13). They sealed this avowal with an oath punctuated with shouts and the playing of instruments. Their sincere pledges of loyalty were met by the Lord's acceptance and his blessing of rest (v. 15).

The seriousness of Asa's reform efforts is reflected in the action he took against his own grandmother Maacah (Heb. reads "mother" but she was actually mother of Abijah, Asa's father; cf. 1 Kings 15:2; 2 Chron. 13:2). He deposed her as queen mother because she had erected an Asherah pole (a stylized image of the fertility goddess). He then destroyed the pole by burning it in the Kidron Valley, just east of Jerusalem (v. 16). The chronicler notes that the reform was not complete, for Asa left the high places intact, but with this single caveat he commends the king for his devotion. On a positive note he observes that Asa brought into the temple silver and gold and various articles that he and his father Abijah had prepared for the purpose (v. 18). These no doubt replaced similar objects that Rehoboam had delivered over to Shishak as tribute payment following Jerusalem's siege by the Egyptians (cf. 12:9). A result of this was the absence of war until the thirty-fifth year of Asa's reign (ca. 876 B.C.; but cf. 16:1 and comments).

3. Asa's Troubles and a Summation (16:1–14)

Though Judah had enjoyed a peaceful relationship with Israel for the first ten years of Asa's reign (14:1), that changed in his thirty-sixth year (ca. 875 B.C.) when Baasha of Israel began to fortify Ramah, a border point strategically located about 6 miles north of Jerusalem (v. 1).

The problem at this point is chronological because Baasha's dates as king are 909–886 B.C. (cf. 1 Kings 15:33). His reign ended, then, ten years or more before Asa's thirty-sixth year and the date of the rebuilding recorded in this passage. The resolution of the problem lies most likely in the assumption that thirty-fifth (15:19) and thirty-sixth (16:1) should rather be read as fifteenth and sixteenth, respectively. The spelling of the

Hebrew words involved would certainly allow this with no difficulty. This means that the Baasha activity occurred in 895 B.C., right after the great convocation at Jerusalem (cf. 15:10).

Perhaps it was this very assembly, with its participants from Israel as well as Judah (15:9), that prompted Baasha to interdict the passage of any more Israelites to Jerusalem. In any event Asa felt so threatened by Baasha's hostile act he immediately entered into treaty relations with Ben-Hadad the Aramean king of Damascus. The terms required Asa to pay silver and gold from the temple and royal treasuries in return for which Ben-Hadad would break off his relations with Israel (vv. 2–3). Asa's appeal rested on the fact that his father (that is, ancestor) had made such a treaty with Ben-Hadad's father so there was strong precedent (cf. 1 Kings 15:18–19).

Ben-Hadad accepted the arrangement, severed the tie with Israel, and attacked certain Israelite cities in the North with the objective of diverting Baasha's attention from his Ramah project in the South (vv. 4–5). The cities he conquered were Ijon, located in Naphtali and 10 miles north of Dan; Dan itself, which lay 25 miles north of the Sea of Galilee; Abel Maim (otherwise known as Abel Beth Maacah; cf. 1 Kings 15:20), just 3 miles west of Dan; and some unnamed store cities of Naphtali.

Forced to withdraw from Ramah, Baasha could not continue his hostilities there. Asa, therefore, moved in, tore down what had been built, and used the stones and timber to create his own fortifications at Geba, just east of Ramah, and Mizpah, between Ramah and Bethel. This would prevent Baasha from making a second effort to fortify Ramah.

Asa had thus used sound human judgment in effecting his kingdom's relief from Israelite threat. But in doing this he had relied on a heathen nation, Damascus, and not on the Lord and had missed the opportunity to punish the Arameans themselves. That very people would return and wage war with Judah through the remaining years of Asa's reign (vv. 7–9).

The message of criticism came from another prophet of the Lord, Hanani the seer. He reminded Asa that God had given victory over Zerah against overwhelming odds (v. 8; cf. 14:9–12) for he was an omnipresent God who ordered all the affairs of human life and history (v. 9). The words of the prophet did not fall on receptive ears, however, and Asa imprisoned Hanani and began oppressive policies against his people (v. 10).

The chronicler closes his account of Asa's reign on a negative note (vv. 11–14). After pointing out that further information concerning Asa could be found in "the book of the kings of Judah and Israel" (an otherwise unknown but noncanonical writing), he draws attention to a foot disease that began to afflict Asa in his thirty-ninth year (ca. 872 B.C.) and that remained with him until his death (v. 12). Though one cannot prove it, there is a likely connection between this incapacity and Asa's lack of reliance on the Lord against Baasha (v. 7) for in his sickness too he depended not on divine but human resources (v. 12).

It is interesting also to note the chronological ramifications of Asa's disease. He died in the forty-first year of his reign, that is, in 870 B.C. This was two years after he became ill (vv. 12–13). His son Jehoshaphat began to reign in 873 indicating that his first three years overlapped the last three of his father. This coregency may well have been necessary because of Asa's debilitation at the end of his life.

D. The Reign of Jehoshaphat (17:1–20:37)

1. Jehoshaphat's Might (17:1–19)

According to 1 Kings 22:41–42, Jehoshaphat began to reign in Ahab's fourth year and he reigned for twenty-five years. A careful reconstruction of Israelite chronology yields the dates of that reign as 873–848 B.C., thus requiring Jehoshaphat's coregency with his father Asa as suggested above.

In order to guard his kingdom against Ahab's hostile intentions, Jehoshaphat manned the various fortified cities and garrisons of Judah as well as the towns of Ephraim captured by his father (vv. 1–2; cf. 11:5; 15:8). He also enjoyed the blessing and protection of the Lord for he walked in the ways of David and repudiated the paganism to which his people so easily succumbed (vv. 3, 6). The people recognized that God was with their king so they lavished their gifts and homage upon him (v. 5).

In his third year (probably the first year of his independent regency, 870 B.C.; cf. 16:12–13), he sent out certain officials, along with Levites and priests, to teach the Book of the Law of the Lord (the Torah or Pentateuch of Moses) to the people of Judah (vv. 7–9). Such a practice had sanction in the Law itself (Lev. 10:11) but it appears to have been done little, if ever, in Israel's past (cf. 2 Chron. 15:3).

Such a move was indicative of Jehoshaphat's godliness and it contributed to his stability and strength. So much was this evident among the surrounding nations they desisted from making war with Judah and, in fact, paid Jehoshaphat voluntary tribute in some cases. The Philistines brought silver and other gifts, and Arab tribes presented him with thousands of rams and goats (vv. 10–11). Israel under Ahab was no longer provocative toward Judah and, indeed, undertook measures to forge cooperative ventures as will presently be seen.

A specific example of Jehoshaphat's might appears in his construction of forts and store cities throughout Judah, which he stocked with abundant provisions and manned with an enormous number of troops (vv. 12–13). From Judah there were 780,000 in all under three commanders and from Benjamin 380,000 under two. The grand total of 1,160,000 is so staggering that many scholars view the figures as referring to technical terminology employed in military contexts. The word "thousand" (Heb. *'eleph*) may also refer to a clan (Judg. 6:15; 1 Sam. 10:19) or even a village (Mic. 5:1). Perhaps, then, Judah provided 780 units of men (*'eleph* being the name of such a unit) and Benjamin 380. If an *'eleph* contained a much smaller actual number of men, 100 for example, the total of 1,160,000 would be correspondingly less. Indeed, 1,160 *'eleph's* could be only 116,000 individuals, still a large number for such a small nation. The problem is exacerbated, moreover, by the fact that these were just the king's men, to be distinguished from others who were stationed in the fortified cities (v. 19).

2. Jehoshaphat and Ahab (18:1–19:3)

When Ahab saw that God had prospered Jehoshaphat and that Jehoshaphat commanded a powerful military force, he sought to achieve an alliance by means of a marriage between his daughter Athaliah and Jehoram, son of Jehoshaphat (v. 1; cf.

21:5–6; 22:2). Evidently this family connection kept the two kingdoms on peaceful terms for most of the years of their respective kings for there is no record of conflict in either Kings or Chronicles.

Toward the end of Ahab's reign (in fact, in his last year, 853 B.C.; cf. 1 Kings 22:1–2; 2 Chron. 18:34), he found himself locked in combat with the Arameans at Ramoth Gilead (1 Kings 22:3), in the Transjordanian desert, 35 miles east of Beth Shan. Meanwhile, Jehoshaphat had paid a visit to Samaria and while there enjoyed a lavish banquet prepared for him by Ahab (vv. 1–2). The motive for the hospitality soon became clear: Ahab wanted Jehoshaphat to join him in his Ramoth Gilead campaign. Having reflected on his commitment to Ahab by virtue of their alliance, Jehoshaphat pledged his full support (v. 3).

There was, however, one precondition. Jehoshaphat must have a clear word from God before he could proceed one way or the other. This seemed a simple matter to Ahab for he had four hundred prophets of whom he could request revelation. Shameless mercenaries that they were, they gave Ahab precisely the word he wanted to hear. "Go," said they, "for God will give it into the king's hand" (v. 5).

Dissatisfied with these false prophets (perhaps prophets of the Canaanite goddess Asherah; cf. 1 Kings 18:19), Jehoshaphat demanded that there be a genuine spokesman for the Lord. Tragically enough, the only one available in all of Samaria, Micaiah son of Imlah, was in prison for his faithful proclamation of truth (v. 7). Ahab knew that it was useless to continue to put Jehoshaphat off so he reluctantly summoned Micaiah from his cell.

While they waited the kings sat by the gate of Samaria observing the charade of the false prophets who dramatized and otherwise attempted to communicate their lying messages (v. 9). One of them, Zedekiah son of Kenaanah, actually took a set of iron horns and like a beast he thrust them this way and that to illustrate the way that Ahab and Jehoshaphat would gore their Aramean enemy (v. 10). As a chorus behind him the other prophets joined in with their words of encouragement. The use of visual aids such as horns was not unusual among even the true prophets of the Lord (cf. Zech. 1:18–21; Jer. 27:2; Ezek.

4:1–3), but mere acting out apart from a sure word from God was empty and meaningless.

As Micaiah made his way to Ahab, his guard told him to prophesy success for that was the unified message of the prophets. True to his calling, however, Micaiah could speak only what God spoke. Thus, when Ahab asked about the chances of victory, Micaiah at first mockingly agreed with the false prophets, a response that was so obviously contrary to what Ahab expected and sensed to be the truth that the king rebuked him and commanded him to be forthright (vv. 14–15).

Micaiah then pronounced the verdict of the Lord (vv. 16–22). Israel was like sheep without a shepherd, he said, so they ought to go home and not attempt such a venture. Chagrined, Ahab turned to Jehoshaphat and said in effect, "I told you so" (v. 17). Micaiah continued, however, and related a vision in which the Lord permitted a lying spirit to inspire the prophets of Ahab to mislead him and lure him into battle, a move that would cost him his life.

The fact that a lying spirit could be permitted by the Lord to do his bidding does not reflect negatively on the person or attributes of God but is rather a statement affirming his absolute sovereignty. Even the demonic hosts are subject to his control and can be allowed to achieve his purposes as the entire Bible abundantly attests (cf. 1 Sam. 16:14; Job 1:12; 2:5–6; Mark 5:1–13; 2 Cor. 12:7).

Stung by this direct contradiction of his lying word, the false prophet Zedekiah lashed out at Micaiah, striking him in the face and asking him derisively to account for the movement of the spirit that allowed him thus to address Micaiah. Zedekiah was convinced that he also spoke by a spirit, and indeed he did, but it was not by the Spirit of God.

The demonic nature of Zedekiah's inspiration would become apparent, Micaiah said, in the day of divine visitation when Zedekiah sought refuge from judgment. Then it would be plain for all to see that he had not spoken the word of the Lord (v. 24).

Ahab also was unconvinced by the message of Micaiah, or if not decided to disregard it. He remanded the prophet to Amon, the mayor of Samaria, and to Joash, called here the "king's son"

(v. 25). This is probably a technical term referring to a high official who represented the king (cf. Jer. 36:26; 38:6; 2 Chron. 28:7). Ahab then ordered that Micaiah be put on a diet of bread and water until he returned safely from the front. Picking up on that arrogant promise of the king, Micaiah predicted that Ahab would return safely only if he had not had a reliable prophetic word. Calling the people to bear witness, he reiterated the message of doom (v. 27).

Soon Ahab and Jehoshaphat found themselves on the field of battle. Ahab disguised himself to avoid detection but instructed Jehoshaphat to retain his royal attire (vv. 28–29). One ought perhaps to give Ahab the benefit of the doubt and assume that he believed that the Arameans would spare Jehoshaphat precisely because they could identify him as the king of Judah.

This seems to find support in the command of the Aramean king to seek out the king of Israel alone (v. 30). In fact, some of his men mistakenly singled out Jehoshaphat and would have killed him had not Jehoshaphat cried out and identified himself. No disguise could frustrate the purpose of the Lord, however, for an arrow randomly shot by an unknown Aramean soldier found its mark between the sections of Ahab's armor, critically wounding the evil king. Courageously he fought on through the day, propping himself up in his chariot until at last he died at the setting of the sun (vv. 33–34).

Jehoshaphat returned to Jerusalem without further incident but had to face yet another prophet, Jehu the son of Hanani (cf. 1 Kings 16:1; 2 Chron. 20:34). Because Jehoshaphat had made alliance with the enemies of the Lord, he said, he also would experience the Lord's judgment (19:1–2; cf. 20:37). On the whole, however, he pleased the Lord for he had purged the Asherah poles out of Judah (v. 3; cf. 17:6).

3. *Jehoshaphat's Judges (19:4–11)*

Early in Jehoshaphat's reign he had begun to send teachers of the Law throughout Judah to instruct his people in the ways of the Lord (17:7–9). Later, possibly after the debacle at Ramoth Gilead, he went personally among the people from Beersheba in the South to the occupied villages of Ephraim in the North

(19:4). His purpose was to turn his subjects back to the Lord, a response no doubt to the rebuke of the prophet Jehu (19:2).

A major part of this effort was to put in place a judicial system free of bribery and partiality. This required judges and other officials who were men of God, persons who themselves were well instructed in the Law and who lived by its principles. Jehoshaphat, therefore, appointed magistrates in all the fortified cities (17:2), charging them to remember that they were ultimately answerable not to man but to God (vv. 5–6). This being the case, they must judge according to the moral and ethical standards of God himself (v. 7).

In Jerusalem Jehoshaphat established a kind of supreme court to which appeal could be made by litigants and judges of the local jurisdictions (vv. 8, 10). The officiants there were Levites, priests, and heads of families (v. 8). Since they had to deal with more difficult and perhaps more important cases, it was incumbent upon them that they serve their fellow citizens in the fear of the Lord and that they impress upon them as well that a criminal act was in fact a sin against the Lord (v. 10).

Amariah the chief priest was in effect the chief justice in matters pertaining to religious life, while Zebadiah son of Ishmael served similarly in civil cases (v. 11). Amariah may be the son of Azariah who was a priest mentioned in connection with Solomon's temple (cf. 1 Chron. 6:10–11). Zebadiah is otherwise unknown but is described here as the leader of the tribe of Judah, probably the governor. The Jerusalem Levites were to be their assistants.

4. Jehoshaphat's Victory Over Moab and Ammon (20:1–30)

Sometime in the last years of Jehoshaphat's reign he was attacked by a coalition of Transjordanian enemies. This quite clearly occurred after Ahab's death and the Battle of Ramoth Gilead in 853 B.C. (20:1; cf. 19:1) but before the death of Ahab's son and successor Ahaziah who died in 852 (cf. 1 Kings 22:51; 2 Chron. 20:35). A date of precisely 852 is reasonable, which would place this narrative four years before Jehoshaphat's death in 848 (cf. 17:1).

The cause of provocation is unknown though it may have

had something to do with Jehoshaphat's participation in the ill-fated Ramoth Gilead campaign. The composition of the enemy host is likewise problematic. It certainly consisted of Moabites and Ammonites and possibly also of Meunites (v. 1). Most Hebrew manuscripts read "Ammonites" twice, a rendition that is meaningless. It seems best to follow the Septuagint "Meunites," a reference to desert peoples who ranged throughout Edom and other areas to the south and southeast of the Dead Sea (cf. 1 Chron. 4:41; 2 Chron. 26:7).

The difficulty is complicated by verse 2, which reads, according to most manuscripts and versions, "a vast army is coming against you from Aram." The NIV and many modern scholars reject "Aram" in favor of "Edom" because of the historical and geographical aspects of the story. Moreover, these two place names are nearly identical in an unpointed (vowelless) text. It would be easy for a scribe to mistake one for the other.

The chronicler says that the enemy troops came "from the other side of the Sea," an obvious allusion to the Dead Sea in light of further reference to Hazazon Tamar, which the historian identifies with En Gedi (v. 2). En Gedi, of course, lay on the western shore of the Dead Sea. Everything would point to these armies as having come from Edom and not Aram.

However, if this attack was in retaliation for Jehoshaphat's involvement in the Israelite campaign against the Arameans at Ramoth Gilead (cf. 18:10), it is not out of the question that the Moabites and Ammonites were serving at the behest of the Arameans and so in that sense were coming "from Aram." The only evidence against this is the later delineation of these antagonists as men of Ammon, Moab, and Mount Seir (vv. 10, 22). The last named are clearly Edomites. It seems best not to draw firm conclusions on the matter.

Jehoshaphat's massive armies notwithstanding (cf. 17:12–19), he was terrified when he learned that enemy troops were already on Judean soil. He convened an assembly from all over Judah for the purpose of fasting and seeking the will of God (vv. 3–4).

Standing before the assembly at the door of the temple, Jehoshaphat addressed the Lord in fervent prayer (vv. 6–12).

He first acknowledged the power and sovereignty of God (v. 6) and then related this very God to Israel's history. It was he who had driven the Canaanites from the land, enabling his own people to establish his name there (vv. 7–8). It was he whom earlier generations had promised to seek in times of need (v. 9; cf. 6:18–39).

Now was such an hour, Jehoshaphat continued. In days of long ago the Lord had forbidden Moses to harm the Ammonites, Moabites, and Edomites (Mount Seir) (cf. Num. 20:17–21), and now these very people were coming to destroy the Lord's inheritance (vv. 10–11). The only hope was in God's miraculous intervention and for that Jehoshaphat pleaded (v. 12).

In a dramatic response the Spirit of God came upon Jahaziel, a Levitical descendant of Asaph (v. 14), and he began to prophesy. He pointed out that the battle was the Lord's, not theirs, so there was no need to fear (v. 15). This was the language of holy war, expressive of the fact that God himself was in charge and was fighting for his own name's sake (cf. 1 Sam. 17:47; 2 Chron. 14:11).

There was, nevertheless, a human strategy. The next day, as Jahaziel instructed, Judah's army should go down to the Pass of Ziz where they would find the enemy at the end of the gorge in the Desert of Jeruel (v. 16). Ziz was the name of a wadi emptying into the Dead Sea just north of En Gedi. The Desert of Jeruel, part of the great Judean wilderness, lay between Hebron and the Dead Sea.

In conformity to the practice of holy war, they were not to engage themselves in battle but were merely to stand aside and watch what God would do (v. 17).

Overwhelmed by the grace and glory of the Lord, Jehoshaphat, the Levites, and the whole assembly could do nothing but fall on their faces before him in worship and then rise to praise his holy name (vv. 18–19).

The next morning they advanced to the Desert of Tekoa, 15 miles south of Jerusalem and at the western end of the Pass of Ziz. Before they even set out, Jehoshaphat had encouraged the people to trust God and his prophets. Then along the way men chosen for the task led Judah's armies in singing the praises of the Lord. Their hymn was one commonly employed in the context of the Lord's covenant grace and salvation (v. 21; cf. Ps. 106:1; 136:1; 1 Chron. 16:34).

Even as the Judeans sang, the Lord brought confusion to the invading armies. The Ammonites and Moabites began to attack the Edomites (men of Mount Seir) and when they had decimated them, they proceeded to slaughter each other (vv. 22–24). When the Judeans arrived at the battle scene, they found only dead bodies and the spoils of war. So vast was the amount of plunder that the men of Jehoshaphat needed three days to gather it together! On the fourth they praised the Lord for all his goodness, a praise that gave the name Beracah to the place (from Heb. *bĕrācāh*, "praise").

With a proper spirit of gratitude Jehoshaphat and his compatriots returned to Jerusalem with unbounded joy. Having arrived at the temple, they once more praised the Lord with their instruments of music (vv. 27–28).

Jehoshaphat's remaining years were peaceful for the nations all around heard of the exploits of Judah's God and were filled with fear lest they, too, should experience his wrath (vv. 29–30).

5. Summation and Last Years (20:31–37)

Consonant with his general approach, the chronicler concludes his account of Jehoshaphat's reign by supplying such information as the king's age when he came to the throne (35), the length of his reign (25 years; 873–848 B.C.), and his mother's name (Azubah daughter of Shilhi). He then offers the assessment that he followed in the righteous footsteps of his father Asa with the exception of failing to remove the high places and being unable to lead his people to unreserved devotion to the Lord (vv. 31–33). For the interested reader, the chronicler suggests a perusal of the annals of Jehu son of Hanani (cf. 19:2) where a full account is available (v. 34).

A final example of an event of Jehoshaphat's reign that might not have been recorded by Jehu was that concerning his disastrous alliance with Ahaziah king of Israel (vv. 35–37). Ahaziah succeeded Ahab in 853 B.C. and reigned for only two years (cf. 1 Kings 22:51).

The treaty between the two kings may have followed Jehoshaphat's victory over the Moabites, Ammonites, and

Edomites just described (20:20–30). Such a triumph would have brought Ezion Geber, a port on the Gulf of Aqaba that normally was under Edomite control, into the hands of Judah once again (cf. 2 Chron. 8:17). Ahaziah would be more than happy to join up with Jehoshaphat in a revival of the maritime industry that had been so important to Solomon (v. 36).

It was this very kind of an alliance with Ahab that had brought divine displeasure upon Jehoshaphat before, however (cf. 19:2), so it is not surprising that a prophet came with a word of rebuke. He was Eliezer son of Dodavahu of Mareshah (v. 37), a man of God mentioned only here. His message was that the Lord would destroy their enterprise, a prediction that came to pass with the destruction of their ships by an unknown cause.

E. The Reign of Jehoram (21:1–20)

Following Jehoshaphat's death and burial with his Davidic royal ancestors, his son Jehoram came to power and reigned for eight years (21:1; cf. v. 5), from 848–841 B.C. (cf. 2 King 8:16–17). His succession appears not to have been smooth and easy for the chronicler says that after Jehoram had "established himself firmly" over Judah, he killed his own brothers and other members of the royal family (v. 4). The fact that the six brothers are named (v. 2) and that they had all received riches and territorial administrations (v. 3) implies that there was a struggle among them all and that it was only because Jehoram was the eldest son that he became king.

Moreover, as the son-in-law of wicked Ahab of Israel (having married Athaliah, daughter of Ahab, v. 6; cf. 2 Kings 8:18, 26–27), Jehoram repudiated the godliness of his father and may have eliminated his brothers in order to establish a rule in opposition to that which had preceded him. The Lord's unconditional covenant with David, however, ensured that the Davidic dynasty would continue despite Jehoram's personal iniquity (v. 7; cf. 2 Sam. 7:12–17; 1 Chron. 17:10–15).

Solomon's unfaithfulness to the Lord had brought untold grief to Israel including the loss of territories (cf. 1 Kings 11:14–40). It is not surprising, then, that Jehoram's disobedience elicited similar results. First Edom rebelled and though Jehoram apparently won a victory over the Edomites he was unable to bring them back under his dominion (vv. 8–10). It will be recalled that Jehoshaphat had outfitted a merchant fleet at Ezion Geber, a traditionally Edomite city (2 Chron. 20:35–37), so the occupation of that city by Jehoshaphat (and probably all of Edom) came to an end under his son.

Libnah, a city located in the lowlands between Judah and Philistia, also revolted and became lost to Jehoram (cf. v. 10). Thus, from both east and west there were breakaway movements that reduced Judah's territorial claims and influence (v. 10b).

Jehoram's covenant disobedience centered specifically in the building of high places and the leading of the people into the sensuous, immoral religious rites (called prostitution by the chronicler, v. 11) associated with the Canaanite fertility cult. This, plus the murder of his brothers, led Elijah the prophet to compose a letter to him in which Elijah chided the king for failing to walk in the ways of Asa and Jehoshaphat and for choosing instead the ways of Ahab (vv. 12–13). This would result, the prophet said, in a divine judgment against the people, the royal family, and the king himself. Jehoram would die an excruciating death occasioned by some kind of bowel disease, such as chronic rectal prolapse (v. 15; cf. vv. 18–19).

The matter of Elijah's letter itself raises certain chronological difficulties since Elijah appears to have ascended to heaven before Joram of Israel began his reign (852 B.C.; cf. 2 Kings 2:1–12; 3:1). Jehoram, however, began his reign, as indicated above, in 848, four years later. The fact that Elijah mentions the death of Jehoram is not a problem here if one grants the possibility of predictive prophecy. The problem lies in the prophet's speaking of Jehoram's bloody purge as an accomplished fact (v. 13).

There are two factors that should be considered in resolving this tension. First, it is clear that Jehoram was co-regent with his father Jehoshaphat for about five years. This is based on the reference in 2 Kings 1:17 to the death of Ahaziah son of Ahab (which occurred in 852; cf. 1 Kings 22:51), who was succeeded by his brother Joram in the second year of Jehoram of Judah (2 Kings 1:17). For the second year of Jehoram to fall in 852, Jehoram must have begun his reign in 853, obviously as co-regent with Jehoshaphat, who did not die until 848. Elijah could, therefore, have written his letter before 852.

The objection to this argument is that the record seems clear in attributing Jehoram's fratricide to a time after Jehoshaphat's death, that is, after 848 (cf. 1 Kings 22:50; 2 Chron. 21:1).

The second factor in support of the integrity of the narrative about Elijah's letter is the lack of evidence that the ascension of the prophet preceded the enthronement of Joram of Israel chronologically. It is well known that the biblical narratives are not always placed in chronological order but frequently appear in thematic or theological sequence. Without decisive data to the contrary, one may well assume that Elijah did not ascend to heaven until after Jehoram became king in 848 and that his letter, therefore, could be that late.

The prediction of judgment came to pass in the form of Philistine and Arab hostility (v. 16). The Arabs in question must have come from the southern area of the Arabian peninsula for they were neighbors of Cushites, a people indigenous not only to Ethiopia but southern Arabia. Both enemies attacked Judah, looted the royal palace, and took captive the king's family except for the youngest son Ahaziah (v. 17; also known as Jehoahaz in 22:1, NASB, KJV). Jehoram then began to suffer as Elijah had prophesied and within two years had died (vv. 18–19).

Contrary to the usual rituals in death and burial (cf. 9:31; 12:16; 14:1; 16:14; 21:1), Jehoram's passing went almost unnoticed. He had no funeral fire in his honor (not a cremation fire but for some other, unknown purpose; cf. 16:14) nor did anyone mourn. And though he was interred in the City of David, he was denied access to the tomb of the kings (v. 20). This honor was only for those who walked in the ways of David and kept covenant with the Lord.

F. The Reign of Ahaziah (22:1–9)

Ahaziah, the sole surviving son of Jehoram, reigned for only one year (841 B.C.; cf. 2 Kings 8:25–26). Perhaps because of Jehoram's incapacity the last two years of his life (21:19), the leaders of Jerusalem placed Ahaziah on the throne (v. 1). They may have done so also to forestall a usurpation of power by Athaliah, Jehoram's Israelite widow and mother of Ahaziah

(v. 2). This she achieved a year later anyway when Ahaziah died at the executioners' hands (vv. 10–12).

The Hebrew text says that Ahaziah was forty-two when he began to reign (v. 2), but this is impossible since his father Jehoram was thirty-two when he came to power and he reigned for only eight years, making him forty at his death (21:5). The correct figure is that of 2 Kings 8:26 which assigns him an age of twenty-two. The younger age would also better account for Ahaziah's being under the care of advisers at the time of his accession (v. 1).

Though Athaliah could not hold the reins directly, she did manage to influence her son to follow the evil course of the northern kingdom from whence she had come (vv. 3–4). He also followed in the footsteps of his grandfather Jehoshaphat by joining Joram king of Israel in a campaign against the Arameans at Ramoth Gilead (v. 5). The Aramean king by then (841 B.C.) was Hazael of Damascus, who had come to power in precisely that year by assassinating Ben-Hadad (cf. 2 Kings 8:7–15). Like Ahab, Joram was wounded and shortly died (2 Kings 9:24). As he lay recuperating at Jezreel, an Israelite royal city in the Plain of Jezreel, Ahaziah visited him (v. 6).

This untimely move cost the Judean king his life for he became caught up in the purge by the new king of Israel, Jehu son of Nimshi, of all the house of Ahab (v. 7; cf. 2 Kings 9:1–10, 21–26). The chronicler explicitly points out that it was the Lord's arrangement of events that brought Ahaziah into those circumstances (v. 7). The outworking of his plan resulted in the death of Judah's royal family and the king himself. Only their respect for the memory of Jehoshaphat prompted Jehu and his men to allow Ahaziah a proper burial (v. 9; cf. 2 Kings 9:28).

The death of Ahaziah and all his family left a power vacuum in Judah that had to filled. This provided his evil mother the opportunity she needed (v. 9).

G. The Inter-Regnum of Athaliah (22:10–23:21)

Athaliah was the daughter of Ahab of Israel and possibly of Jezebel, princess of Sidon (cf. 1 Kings 16:31; 2 Kings 8:18, 26). She had married Jehoram son of Jehoshaphat and was largely responsible for his defection from the Lord (2 Chron. 21:6).

Their son was Ahaziah who, with his uncle Joram the king of
Israel, had perished at the hand of the next Israelite king, Jehu
(22:7–9).

With her son and most of the royal family of Judah dead,
Athaliah moved to install herself as regent by slaughtering
whatever remnant of the Davidic family remained in Jerusalem
(v. 10). This meant, of course, that she murdered her own
kinfolk. Her object appears to have been the introduction of
Israelite idolatry into Judah and possibly the reunification of the
two kingdoms under the headship of the Omride dynasty (cf.
2 Kings 8:26 where Athaliah is called "daughter of Omri" in the
sense of affiliation with that royal house).

Her plot was undermined, however, by Jehosheba, daughter of King Jehoram (and possibly of Athaliah herself), who took
away Ahaziah's infant son Joash and hid him from his murderous
grandmother. The narrator points out that this could be done
because Jehosheba, wife of Ahaziah and therefore aunt of the
baby boy, was also the wife of the high priest Jehoiada, who
provided sanctuary for them in the temple (vv. 11–12). There
they remained throughout the six years of Athaliah's reign.

In the seventh year (now 835 B.C.) Jehoiada organized a
conspiracy against Athaliah designed to rid the kingdom of her
and restore the Davidic dynasty to young Joash. This called for
the participation of military officers (23:1), Levitical leaders, and
clan chiefs from all over the land (v. 2). When he had assembled
them at the temple, Jehoiada led them in a ceremony of
covenant affirmation in which they recognized the legitimacy of
Joash to reign as the Davidic offspring (v. 3).

Then he outlined the strategy. A third of the priests and
Levites would guard the doors of the temple, a third would be at
the royal palace, and a third at the Foundation Gate (cf. 2 Kings
11:6 where it is called the Sur Gate; Heb *sûr* means "turning
aside"). Other men would gather in the temple courtyards. The
idea was to prevent access to the temple to anyone but
officiating priests and Levites and to guard the person of the
young king (vv. 4–7).

When all was arranged and the soldiers were armed with
the temple weapons of David (cf. 2 Sam. 8:7), Jehoiada led
Joash out to the assembly, crowned him, presented him with the

protocols of his office as king—a copy of the covenant (cf. Deut. 17:18–20), and anointed him (cf. 1 Sam. 16:13). Then the crowd burst out with the acclamation "Long live the king!" (vv. 8–11).

Too late, Athaliah realized what had happened and came out of her palace to view the festivities of coronation. Immediately she understood that her regency had come to an end in a coup led by the religious and military leadership of the nation. All she could do was tear her clothing in frustration and despair and cry out "Treason!" (v. 13). Showing no mercy, Jehoiada ordered the villainous queen to be dragged from the sacred temple precincts to the Horse Gate near the palace. There his executioners put her to death (v. 15).

A second covenant ceremony followed. This was for the purpose of joining priest, people, and king in a solemn compact to be the people of the Lord exclusively (v. 17). This done, they dramatized that commitment by demolishing the Baal temple with its altars and images and they slew Mattan the priest of Baal (cf. Deut. 13:6–11; 1 Kings 18:40; 2 Kings 10:25–28). Then Jehoiada restored the ministry of the temple to authorized priestly and Levitical personnel, those qualified under the Law to offer its sacrifices and perform other functions. To safeguard the purity and sanctity of the temple and its worship Jehoiada stationed doorkeepers there to allow only properly certified officiants to enter (vv. 16–19).

Finally young Joash made his way from the temple through the Upper Gate and to the palace grounds. The Upper Gate (cf. 27:3) was evidently between the temple and palace, suggesting a large complex of public buildings embracing both structures (v. 20; cf. 1 Kings 3:1; 6:37–7:8). When he arrived at the palace, he sat upon the throne of David, thus completing the last formal act of succession. Once more the crowd shouted its approval and the land was at rest. The spiritual decline brought by the ungodly reigns of Jehoram and Ahaziah and the usurpation of Athaliah had come to an end after thirteen long years (848–835).

H. The Reign of Joash (24:1–27)

Joash was only a year old when he had been hidden in the temple. Now, six years later and after the death of his grandmother Athaliah, he became king at the age of seven, reigning for forty years (835–796 B.C.). Jehoiada the priest, who was his uncle and guardian (cf. 22:11), guided him in his early years and was obviously influential in determining the course of his reign (vv. 2–3, 12, 14, 17–18).

Indicative of this influence was the fact that Jehoiada selected two wives for Joash (v. 3) and without doubt encouraged him in the task of temple restoration (vv. 4–7). To accomplish this, the king ordered the priests and Levites to travel throughout the towns and villages of the kingdom to collect the temple taxes required by the Law (cf. Exod. 30:12–16). For some reason they were not quick to obey so the zealous young monarch impatiently summoned the priest and chided him for the delay in implementing his orders. Wicked Athaliah had desecrated the temple and Joash was eager to restore it to its pristine purity (v. 7).

To expedite matters, Joash arranged for a chest to be placed at the gate of the temple so that contributions could be made to the project of refurbishing it. He then commanded the people to come and pay the temple tax, an appeal that was met with resounding success. Over and over again it was filled with the contributions of the leaders and populace alike (vv. 8–11).

Joash and Jehoiada then turned the proceeds over to the supervisors of construction who hired masons, carpenters, and metalworkers to undertake the work (v. 12). The project went apace until at last the temple resembled its original design and was even better built than the first. Amazingly, the work was accomplished at a cost under estimate and the leftover funds came back to Joash and Jehoiada. They used the silver and gold to make articles and vessels required for the temple services. As long as the high priest Jehoiada lived the spirit of revival continued on and the people resorted to the house of the Lord for worship (vv. 13–14).

At last Jehoiada died at the age of 130 (v. 15). Because of his piety, his efforts at reformation, and his role as tutor to the king, he was buried among the kings in the city of David (v. 16). It was not long, however, before leaders of Judah influenced the king to abandon the worship of the Lord and return to the heathenism of their fathers (v. 18; cf. 2 Chron. 12:14; 20:33; 21:11; 22:3–5).

True to his covenant love, the Lord sent prophets to warn his people and encourage them to repent, but to no avail (v. 19). He, therefore, raised up Zechariah son of Jehoiada the priest, filled him with his Spirit, and placed upon his lips a message of divine judgment. His people had forsaken him so the Lord would forsake them and, indeed, already had (v. 20). Disregarding the fact that they stood as it were on holy ground just outside the temple, a band of thugs stoned the godly prophet to death by instruction of the king.

Zechariah was not only the son of Joash's mentor Jehoiada, to whom the king owed everything (cf. v. 22), but he was also Joash's cousin since Jehoiada was husband of Joash's aunt (cf. 22:11). Thus the involvement of the king in this martyrdom was all the more reprehensible. In fact, the death of Zechariah was so outrageous it may be he to whom Jesus referred when he spoke of the death of all the prophets from Abel to Zechariah (Matt. 23:34–35).

Against this interpretation is the fact that Jesus identified Zechariah as "the son of Berekiah" (Zech. 1:1). The difficulty here is that nothing is known of the martyrdom of this Zechariah, while the other died in circumstances much in keeping with Jesus' description. Probably it is impossible to resolve the matter one way or the other.

As the prophet died he uttered a curse against Joash (v. 22), a curse that apparently came to bear very quickly in an Aramean invasion of Judah at the beginning of the next year. Jerusalem was besieged, the leaders of Judah were slain, and the enemy carried off plunder to Damascus. All this happened despite the numerical superiority of the Judeans because the Lord was punishing his people (vv. 23–24).

Joash, though wounded, was not claimed by the Arameans. A band of zealots from among his own servants rose up against him, however, and slew him in his bed (v. 25). They did so because of their commitment to the ideals of Jehoiada whose son Zechariah had been struck down by order of the king. Ironically, Jehoiada, who was not a king, was buried in the royal tombs (24:16), while Joash, who was a king, was not (v. 25). The account of the conspiracy in 2 Kings 12:21 names the assassins (though with variant spellings) but does not indicate their nationality. An interesting insight into the chronicler's approach appears in his description of the killers as an Ammonite and Moabite respectively. He obviously wished to attribute this death of a Davidic king (even an evil one) to someone other than a native son.

More information on Joash and his reign is available, the chronicler notes in closing, in a volume known as "the annotations on the book of the kings" (v. 27), perhaps the canonical Old Testament books of 1 and 2 Kings.

I. The Reign of Amaziah (25:1–28)

Amaziah, son of Joash, reigned for twenty-nine years, from 796 to 767 B.C. (v. 1; cf. 2 Kings 14:1). Though the chronicler's assessment of him is generally favorable, he does note that Amaziah's obedience to the Lord was not wholehearted (v. 2).

Once he had secured the kingdom firmly under his control, Amaziah avenged his father's murder by slaying its perpetrators. He left their children alive, however, because of the teaching of the Mosaic law that children must not be punished for the misdeeds of their parents (vv. 3–4; cf. Deut. 24:16). In this way he illustrated his godly spirit.

The time came when Amaziah decided to go to war with Edom, perhaps once more to gain access to the seaport on the Gulf of Aqaba (cf. 2 Kings 14:1–22). To launch such an ambitious enterprise required the conscription of a large military host so Amaziah mustered 300,000 men twenty years old and up from Judah and Benjamin. Also, he hired 100,000 Israelites for one hundred talents (ca. 3 3/4 tons) of silver (vv. 5–6).

This alliance displeased the Lord, however, so he sent a prophet to urge Amaziah to break off the arrangement. Even such an enormous army would come to ruin if made up of an unholy coalition, he said. It was the Lord, after all, who gave victory or brought defeat (vv. 7–8; cf. 19:1–2).

Amaziah was convinced but since he had already paid the silver he was reluctant to draw back and forfeit it. The prophet assured him that God could more than make up for the petty loss so Amaziah sent his Israelite mercenaries home. Though they had gotten their pay without having fought to earn it, the

Israelite soldiers were angry because they thirsted for the adventure of combat and, more importantly, would not share in any spoils of victory (vv. 9–10).

Ready at last, the Judean troops set out from Edom. Before reaching their destination they encountered the men of Seir (that is, the Edomites; cf. 20:2, 22) at the Valley of Salt, most likely the region to the south end of the Dead Sea (cf. 2 Sam. 8:13; 2 Kings 14:7). The outcome of the battle was the immediate death of 10,000 Edomites and the slaughter of 10,000 others by casting them alive from a cliff (vv. 11–12).

The joy of triumph was mitigated, however, by the fact that the Israelite soldiers of fortune who had been sent home looted and pillaged all along the way (v. 13). They killed 3,000 Judeans and, in an action that revealed their true motives in coming to Amaziah's aid, they plundered from the Judeans what they were denied from the Edomites.

Meanwhile, Amaziah returned to Jerusalem carrying with him the idols of Edom to which he evidently attributed his success (v. 14; cf. 28:23). Again a prophet came to him (cf. v. 7) and asked how it was that he could worship gods that could not even deliver their own people from disaster. In a rage Amaziah rebuked the prophet, reminding him that he had no business speaking since he was not an appointee of the king (v. 16; cf. 18:6–7; Amos 7:12–13). Chastened by this severe response, the prophet ceased his admonition but not before prophesying that Amaziah would come to an untimely end. Still stinging from the treachery of the Israelites (v. 13), Amaziah decided to confront their King Jehoash (sometimes spelled Joash) and punish him for the evil his nation had inflicted on Judah's unprotected villages. Jehoash, who reigned from 798 to 783 (cf. 2 Kings 13:10), was the son of Jehoahaz and grandson of Jehu (v. 17), the Israelite rebel responsible for the death of Ahaziah, grandfather of Amaziah (cf. 22:9).

Jehoash replied to the challenge by reciting a parable in which a thistle requested of a cedar that the cedar give his daughter in marriage to the son of the thistle. A wild animal then came along and trampled the thistle into the ground (v. 18). Jehoash explained the parable by comparing little Judah to the thistle, proud because it had subdued Edom in battle. Such arrogance, however, against Israel, the mighty cedar tree, would be met by a crushing defeat at the hands of Israel's army, the wild beast (v. 19).

Unfazed, Amaziah attacked, thus playing into the hands of the Lord who had brought the confrontation to pass to punish Judah for its idolatry (v. 20; cf. v. 14). The field of battle was at Beth Shemesh, a Judean town 20 miles due west of Jerusalem. As prophesied, Judah was defeated. Amaziah fell prisoner to Jehoash who took him back to Jerusalem. The Israelites then broke down the city walls from the Ephraim Gate (cf. Neh. 8:16) to the Corner Gate (cf. Jer. 31:38), a distance of 400 cubits (about 600 feet). This gave them access to the temple and palace area from which they looted gold, silver, and other articles under the care of Obed-Edom (cf. 1 Chron. 26:15, where the temple storehouse was assigned to the Obed-Edom family). Certain hostages also went north with the victors including possibly Amaziah himself (vv. 23–24).

Whether or not Amaziah went as prisoner to Samaria he ended up in Jerusalem, outliving Jehoash of Israel by fifteen years. But things did not go well with him there for ever since his defection from the Lord (vv. 14–16) Amaziah had become the target of conservative elements who were eager to replace him. Eventually he fled to Lachish, 30 miles southwest of Jerusalem, where he finally fell victim to his relentless pursuers (v. 27). Like his father Joash before him, he perished at the hands of assassins (cf. 24:24) and also like him he evidently was denied burial in the royal tombs, though his body was returned to Jerusalem (here called the city of Judah, v. 28).

Further information on Amaziah from the beginning to the end of his reign is available, the chronicler notes, "in the book of the kings of Judah and Israel" (v. 26), probably a reference to the biblical Books of 1 and 2 Kings.

For Further Study

1. The chronicler organizes his history of the Divided Monarchy around the Davidic dynasty. How does he make this clear in this chapter?

2. What are the principles involved in reconstructing and interpreting the chronological data of the Divided Monarchy

period? For a clear presentation see Edwin R. Thiele, *The Mysterious Numbers of the Hebrew Kings* (Grand Rapids: Eerdmans).

3. Elijah and Elisha, prominently featured in 1 and 2 Kings, play little or no role in Chronicles. What does this say about the chronicler's historical and theological method?

4. What are the principles of belief and behavior which, if followed, brought God's blessing and favor to the kings of Judah and which, if violated, brought his judgment? How relevant are these to modern Christian faith and conduct?

Chapter 6

The Dynasty of David: Uzziah to the Restoration Community

(2 Chronicles 26:1–36:23)

A. The Reign of Uzziah (26:1–23)

The parallel accounts of Uzziah's reign (here and 2 Kings 15:1–7) both seem to suggest that he was sixteen when he succeeded his father Amaziah upon the death of the latter (v. 1). He then went on to reign for fifty-two years (v. 3; cf. 2 Kings 15:2).

There are many problems with this interpretation, which must be addressed. First, it is clear that the terminal date of Uzziah (also known as Azariah; cf. 2 Kings 14:21) is 739 B.C. (cf. 2 Kings 15:1, 8, 13, 17, 23, 27). A fifty-two-year reign would put his first year, therefore, at 790 B.C. However, Amaziah reigned from 796–767 (cf. 25:1) or twenty-three years past what seems to be Uzziah's first year, 790. As most scholars recognize, the period from 790–767 must represent a time of co-regency in which Amaziah and Uzziah shared power. This necessitates the view that Uzziah's age of sixteen is referring to his commencement of co-regency in 790 and not sole regency in 767 for he could not rule in any sense for fifty-two years after 767.

In support of this is the fact that Uzziah "sought God during the days of Zechariah" (v. 5), without question the Zechariah son of Jehoiada who had been martyred under King Joash (24:20–22). Joash died in 796 so Zechariah's death also occurred before that. For Uzziah to have learned at Zechariah's feet, he must have been of teachable age before 796. If he was sixteen in 790 he would have been born in 806 and would have been ten when Joash died in 796. He could easily have been Zechariah's pupil before that prophet's death but only if his age of sixteen refers to the time of co-regency.

The implications of all this are revealing. It seems that Amaziah's decline began within his first six years (796–790; cf. 25:7, 14–16) and that "the people of Judah" (meaning the strong leadership, v. 1; cf. 22:1) took steps to prepare for his succession (or perhaps even replacement; cf. 25:27) by appointing his young son Uzziah as co-regent. The statement that they "made him king in place of his father" (v. 1) turned out to mean only that the people viewed Uzziah as the eventual successor to Amaziah, a development that actually came to pass many years later upon Amaziah's death.

The events of his reign recorded by the chronicler transpired in the course of Uzziah's independent regency from 767 to 739. This is specifically stated in 26:2 where the author says that Uzziah rebuilt Elath and restored it to Judah after his father's death. As has been seen Elath (or Ezion Geber), and Edom generally, fluctuated between independence and Judean control repeatedly (cf. 2 Chron. 8:17; 20:36; 21:8–10).

As long as Uzziah sought the Lord he prospered (v. 5). This pertained to military affairs as well as other enterprises. He invaded Philistia; broke down the defenses of Gath, Jabneh (also known as Jabneel; cf. Joash 15:11), and Ashdod; and rebuilt other towns near Ashdod and elsewhere throughout Philistine territory, probably as fortresses (v. 6). He also attacked a Philistine and Arabian force at Gur Baal (7 or 8 miles east of Beersheba) and some Meunites at an unknown location (v. 7; cf. 20:1). Such exploits caused the Ammonites east of the Jordan to become alarmed so they brought Uzziah tribute (v. 8). To the border of Egypt itself Uzziah's reputation spread.

Defensively, Uzziah fortified Jerusalem by constructing towers at the Corner Gate (cf. 25:23), the Valley Gate (cf. Neh. 2:13, 15), and "at the angle of the wall" (v. 9; cf. Neh. 3:19–20, 24–25). These areas were all apparently on the west side of the city. Effort was also expended in the Negev desert where Uzziah built defensive posts and dug cisterns to provide water for his livestock located there and in the hill country and plains. Throughout the country he established extensive agricultural industries because, as the chronicler poignantly observes, "he loved the soil" (v. 10).

His offensive and defensive policies required a large military force so Uzziah, much like David before him (cf. 1 Chron. 27:1–15), organized his fighting men by divisions under the command of family (or clan) leaders. There were 2,600 of these officers and a total of 307,500 men under them (vv. 12–13). Hananiah, a royal official, was assisted by Jeiel the secretary and Maaseiah the officer in the work of mustering and assigning all these troops (v. 11).

Nor did the army lack for the best equipment. In addition to the normal armor and weaponry, they enjoyed the use of such sophisticated devices as "artillery" pieces designed to fire projectiles of arrows and stones (vv. 14–15). This only enhanced Uzziah's reputation all the more for he became celebrated far and wide as a king of great power.

This very might became the means of his fall, however, for his leadership in military and political life led him to believe that he could dominate the realm of the religious as well. It is true, of course, that the Davidic king by virtue of his covenant relationship to the Lord could undertake certain priestly privileges (cf. 1 Chron. 13:1–8; 15:1–15). These did not extend to the offering of incense, however, a rite that was reserved to the Aaronic priesthood alone (Exod. 30:7–8). Uzziah thus overstepped his bounds and went into the temple to burn incense (v. 16).

Indignant over this breach of authority and protocol, Azariah the high priest took eighty of his priestly colleagues into the temple to confront the king with his sacrilege. What he was doing, they said, was a violation of the clear teaching of the Law in such matters (v. 18). He must leave the temple at once.

Rather than submit, Uzziah became angry, a response that provoked the wrath of God upon him. At once his forehead became leprous, a condition that rendered him ceremonially unclean and unfit to function cultically or even socially (cf. Lev. 13). The priests and Uzziah himself recognized the gravity of the situation and left the sacred precincts in great haste (v. 20).

No longer could the king effectively perform his responsibilities. In fact, he was quarantined to a separate, private dwelling place apart from both temple and palace (v. 21). His son Jotham stepped in to run the affairs of state (cf. 27:1) until Uzziah died. Even after death the king was segregated from his family for as a leper he could not be buried with them (v. 23). His remains ended up in a field belonging to the crown but not in the royal cemetery (cf. 21:20; 24:25).

Finally, the historian urges those interested in further information about Uzziah to consult the prophet Isaiah. The few remarks in that prophet's book (cf. Isa. 1:1; 6:1) leads one to believe that Isaiah may have composed another work in which Uzziah figured more prominently.

B. The Reign of Jotham (27:1–9)

Jotham, who reigned for sixteen years, began to do so in 750 B.C., eleven years before his father's death (v. 1; cf. 2 Kings 15:32–33). Eleven years, then, were spent as co-regent, a tenure necessary because of Uzziah's segregation from society and government (26:21). Jotham, therefore, reigned for only five years as independent king, until 735.

He was essentially a godly ruler as his father had been. In fact, he had learned from his father the folly of exceeding his limits of authority and desisted from violating the temple (cf. 26:16). In spite of his good example, however, the people of the land continued their covenant infidelity (v. 2).

Among Jotham's accomplishments were the rebuilding of the Upper Gate of the temple (cf. 23:20), construction on the wall surrounding the hill of Ophel (the old Jebusite city), and the placement of towns in the hill country and forts and towers in the forest lands (vv. 3–4).

The Ammonites, who had been forced to pay tribute to Uzziah (cf. 26:8), evidently had ceased doing so and had to be brought to attention by Jotham. He imposed the heavy tax of a hundred talents (ca. 3 3/4 tons) of silver, 10,000 cors (ca. 62,000 bushels) of wheat, and the same amount of barley. This they paid for at least three years (v. 5).

The success of Jotham's reign the chronicler attributes to his devotion to the Lord (v. 6). Further record of all this he says was preserved in "the book of the kings of Israel and Judah" (v. 7), very likely the biblical Books of 1 and 2 Kings. His age at accession (25) plus the years of reign (16) add up to a brief life span of forty-one years. The sixteen years do not include four more of a co-regency with his son Ahaz, however, making a total of about forty-five. At his death Jotham was accorded an honorable burial with his Davidic ancestors in the tombs of the kings (vv. 8–9).

C. The Reign of Ahaz (28:1–27)

Ahaz, whose sole regency commenced in 731 B.C., reigned with his father Jotham for four years (735–731), a period that appears to be credited to neither one. This conclusion is based on the fact that Jotham reigned for at least sixteen years, his first year without any doubt being 750 B.C. (cf. 27:1). On the other hand, Ahaz reigned for sixteen years as well (v. 1), his last year, as all scholars agree, being 715 B.C. (cf. 2 Kings 16:1–2; 2 Chron. 29:1; 2 Kings 18:13). This requires an accession date for Ahaz of 731. The years 735–731, then, were years of dual regency, for Jotham also is assigned at least twenty years in another passage (thus 750–731; cf. 2 Kings 15:30).

More important than (but not unrelated to) these matters of chronology is the devastating judgment of the chronicler concerning the rule of Ahaz (vv. 1b–4). He contradicted all that David represented and followed the ways of his fellow kings of Israel to the North. He made idols, burned human sacrifices (including his own sons) in the Valley of Ben Hinnom, and offered sacrifices and burned incense at every kind of heathen shrine.

Ben Hinnom refers to a valley just west of Mount Zion that served as a dumping ground in ancient times. Because of its association with impurities burned there, it became synonymous with impurity itself. Moreover, it was the site of idolatrous worship, particularly the offering up of children to the Ammonite god Molech (Lev. 18:21; 20:2–5; Deut. 12:31; 2 Kings 23:10; Jer. 7:31–32; 19:2, 6; 32:35). The name in Hebrew, *gê' hinnōm*, gave rise to the form Gehenna, a term used to describe hell (cf. Matt. 5:22).

Such abomination could not go unchecked and unpunished so the Lord raised up Rezin king of Aram (v. 5; cf. 2 Kings 16:5) who invaded Jerusalem, defeated Ahaz, and took many prisoners to Damascus. His ally in this operation was none other than Pekah king of Israel who killed 120,000 Judean soldiers in one day. These included some of Ahaz's own choice men such as his son Maaseiah, his palace manager Azrikam, and his chief official Elkanah (vv. 6–7). In addition, the Israelites took as prisoners 200,000 wives and children and a great amount of spoil (v. 8).

This signal triumph did not meet with unanimous approval, however, for when Pekah's armies arrived back in Samaria they were accosted by Oded the prophet (mentioned only here) who reminded them that though the Lord had chosen them to be his instrument of judgment against Judah, they had slaughtered them mercilessly and beyond expectation (v. 9). Worse still, they had brought back their own Judean brothers with the intent of enslaving them. How could they consider doing such a thing when they themselves were such sinners? The only remedy, Oded concluded, was to send the captives back to Judah (vv. 10–11).

The word of the prophet was reinforced by four of Ephraim's (that is, Israel's) leaders who also ordered that the prisoners be returned lest the wrath of God visit them (vv. 12–13). In the face of such dire warnings the army commanders ordered that the prisoners and their possessions be returned. They supplied them with clothing, food, and medicines and even donkeys for those too weak to walk. Then for reasons not specified they took them to Jericho where they once more were among their own people (vv. 12–15).

It had become clear to Ahaz by now that he was no match for the forces that threatened him on every side. Israel, it is true, had softened toward Judah to the extent of returning prisoners of war but it was Israel also that had decimated Judah's army in that war (v. 6). Ahaz had every right to continue to fear his northern neighbor.

More immediately pressing were attacks by the Edomites and Philistines. The latter managed to capture Judean towns in the Negev and lowlands (the Shepelah) including Beth Shemesh, Aijalon, Gederoth (or Gederah), Soco, Timnah, and Gimzo—all important border settlements guarding valleys leading into Judah. This all came about because Ahaz had been disobedient to the Lord (v. 19).

Rather than turn to the Lord for help Ahaz looked to Assyria, the great Mesopotamian nation that was beginning to dominate the entire eastern world (v. 16). The Assyrian king then in power was Tiglath-Pileser III (745–727 B.C.). Despite the implicit warnings of Isaiah the prophet to have nothing to do with the Assyrians (Isa. 7:4–9), Ahaz hired Tiglath-Pileser by paying him from the assets of the temple, the palace, and even private monies of his princes (v. 21). It was to no avail, however, for Tiglath-Pileser gave Judah more trouble than help, though 2 Kings 16:9 reveals that Damascus, Judah's enemy, fell to the Assyrians.

The trouble that came as a result of these entanglements was in the spiritual and not the political or military area of life. Reflecting on his defeat by the Arameans (v. 5), Ahaz concluded that the gods of Damascus must be superior to the Lord God of Israel. He therefore began to worship them by the offering of sacrifices (v. 23; cf. 2 Kings 16:10–16). What is so ironic and baffling about the whole thing is the fact that Ahaz began to adopt the Aramean cult after Damascus itself had fallen to the Assyrians (2 Kings 16:9–10). Only total spiritual blindness could account for the rejection of the Lord because of Judah's defeat by the Arameans and then the embracing of the Aramean gods despite the fall of Damascus to a superior power, Assyria.

In any event, Ahaz was consistent at least in his repudiation of the worship of the true God for he robbed the temple of its furnishings, shut its doors, and erected his pagan altars on the street corners of Jerusalem (v. 24). Throughout Judah he set up shrines at high places, a sacrilege that provoked the Lord to anger.

The chronicler concludes his account of Ahaz and his wicked reign by drawing attention to further information to be found in "the book of the kings of Judah and Israel" (v. 26), likely the biblical Books of 1 and 2 Kings (cf. 2 Kings 16). He notes also that Ahaz, like Jehoram (21:20), Joash (24:25), and Uzziah (26:23) before him, was buried in Jerusalem but not in the royal tombs (v. 27).

D. The Reign of Hezekiah (29:1–32:33)

1. The Restoration of the Temple (29:1–36)

The narrative of the reign of Hezekiah raises once more a chronological complication that must be addressed at least briefly. It was noted with reference to Ahaz that he occupied Judah's throne until 715 B.C. (28:1). The chronicler (in agreement with 2 Kings 18:1–3) says that Hezekiah reigned for twenty-nine years (29:1), a period that all scholars agree ended in 686 B.C. Thus, it appears that Hezekiah immediately followed his father in 715 and ruled for twenty-nine years, until 686.

The problem is that 2 Kings 18:1 commences Hezekiah's tenure in the third year of Hoshea of Israel, which would be about 729–28. Other events such as the invasion of Samaria by Shalmaneser IV of Assyria (727–722) in Hezekiah's fourth year (2 Kings 18:9), which was 725 B.C., support an earlier accession date as well. On the other hand, Sennacherib (705–681) laid siege to Jerusalem in Hezekiah's fourteenth year (2 Kings 18:13), which clearly has to be fourteen years after 715 (or 701, as all scholars agree) since Sennacherib did not reign until after 715.

The resolution lies in positing a co-regency between Ahaz and Hezekiah from 729–28 to 715 and an independent reign for Hezekiah thereafter until 686. Though the Kings account mentions some events of the co-regency period, the chronicler appears to have confined his record to the sole regency, that is, to the 715–686 era.

Contrary to Ahaz, Hezekiah was a godly king, walking in the steps of his ancestor David (v. 2). Confirmation of this is evident in his very first year (715 B.C.) when in his first month he reopened the temple and undertook badly needed repairs. Assembling the priests and Levites in the eastern courtyard of the temple, he commanded that they consecrate themselves and the temple, remove from it the things that defiled it (that is, the paraphernalia of heathen worship; cf. 2 Kings 18:4), and reestablish the worship of the Lord, which their fathers had neglected and even repudiated (vv. 5–7).

The result of the apostasy had been vividly demonstrated by the judgment of the Lord. He had made his people an object of scorn, he had slain them in war, and had allowed many of them to be carried off as prisoners (v. 8; cf. 28:5–8). The only remedy was a wholehearted return to the Lord, a return marked by covenant renewal (cf. 23:16) and religious purity and devotion (vv. 10–11).

Obediently the Levites set to work under the leadership of Mahath and Joel who represented the Kohathites, Kish and Azariah of the Merarites, and Joah and Eden of the Gershonites (v. 12). Cooperating with them were descendants of Elizaphan (otherwise unknown), Shimri and Jeiel. There were also the Asaphites, Zechariah and Mattaniah; Hemanites, Jehiel and Shimei; and Jeduthunites, Shemaiah and Uzziel (vv. 13–14). These with their assistants entered the temple and brought out all the impurities, carrying them to the place of burning in the Kidron Valley east of Jerusalem (vv. 15–16; cf. 15:16).

All this housecleaning had commenced on the first day of the first month (evidently the first month of Hezekiah's reign and not of the year itself; cf. v. 3) and continued for eight days. When it was done, the ceremony of consecration went on for eight more days until at last on the sixteenth day all was complete (v. 17). The Levites then reported to the king that the temple was purified, its furnishings that Ahaz had removed and desecrated were repaired and rededicated, and everything stood ready for the resumption of temple worship (vv. 18–19).

The next day Hezekiah took the leadership of Jerusalem with him to the temple and offered on behalf of the kingdom, the temple, and Judah twenty-eight sacrificial animals appropriate to burnt and sin offerings (vv. 20–21; cf. Lev. 1–6). The distinction between the kingdom and Judah is that the kingdom refers to the political, royal aspect of the nation, while Judah refers to the population (cf. v. 24 where Israel also is included). The bulls, rams, and lambs were for burnt offerings (v. 22; cf. Lev. 1:3–13), the purpose of which was to atone for sins generally. The goats were for sin offerings (vv. 23–24; cf. Lev. 4:1–5:13), the purpose of which was to atone for specific sins. There were seven of each kind of animal to show the completeness and perfection of the nation's repentance.

In preparation for the ritual of sacrifice, Hezekiah had stationed the Levitical musicians in the appropriate places in the temple area for them to play their instruments. This was all done according to specifications outlined long before by David and his two principal prophetical advisers, Gad and Nathan (cf. 1 Chron. 25:1, 6), though the role of the two prophets in this respect is nowhere else cited.

As the sacrificing began, the Levites proceeded to sing and play their instruments while the multitudes of the people stood by with bowed heads. This accompaniment of praise and submission continued all through the service until the last sacrifice had been offered (vv. 27–28). Then king and people alike fell to their knees and worshiped as the Levites praised the Lord with the psalms of David and Asaph (vv. 29–30).

Now that the corporate sacrifices for the monarchy, temple, and citizenry had been completed, Hezekiah invited individuals, now qualified because of the atonement just rendered, to come privately with their offerings. These were in the form of burnt and thank offerings, sacrifices made in recognition of an existing state of peace and fellowship between God and man (v. 31; cf. Lev. 3:1–17; 7:11–36).

The number of burnt offerings was 70 bulls, 100 rams, and 200 male lambs, while the peace offerings totaled 600 bulls and 3,000 sheep and goats. So lavish was the people's response that the few priests could not care for all the sacrifices and had to press their Levitical assistants into service until other priests could be properly consecrated for the task (vv. 32–34).

In less than a month the temple was cleansed and consecrated and the structures of worship were once again put in place. Hezekiah and his people saw in this speed of accomplishment the hand of the Lord and for this they rejoiced (vv. 35–36).

2. The Great Passover (30:1–31:1)

In what in all probability was his first year, Hezekiah made preparations for the greatest Passover held in Israel since the days of Solomon (30:26). He sent couriers throughout Israel and Judah, as far afield as the outer reaches of Ephraim and Manasseh, inviting the faithful to come to observe the festival. Since there were too few priests who were properly consecrated by the first month (that is, the first month of the religious calendar or Nisan; cf. Exod. 12:1–2; Esth. 3:7) Hezekiah decided to schedule it on the second, about April/May according to modern calendars (cf. Num. 9:11).

From Beersheba in the deep South to Dan in the far North, the invitation went forth with the full backing of the people of Jerusalem as well as the king (vv. 4–5). With earnest appeal they encouraged their brethren to return to the Lord so that he would return to those of them who had survived the deportation of the Assyrians (v. 6). Though the chronicler had made no reference to it, the Assyrian captivity had taken place in the ninth year of Hoshea king of Israel (that is, 722 B.C.; cf. 2 Kings 17:6), which would have been in the sixth year of Hezekiah's co-regency with Ahaz (cf. 2 Kings 18:1).

Those survivors, Hezekiah said, ought all the more to return to the Lord and demonstrate their repentance by attending the Passover and making commitment to covenant obedience (vv. 7–8). To do so, he continued, might even bring God's blessing upon their captive brethren and hasten their return from exile. Faithfulness to the Lord would elicit faithfulness from the Lord (v. 9).

The messengers faithfully carried out their assignment, traveling as far as Zebulun in Galilee, but with little success. Most of the people treated the solicitation with contempt though a few from such distant points as Asher, Manasseh, and Zebulun swallowed their pride and sought the face of the Lord in Jerusalem. It may be their very remoteness from Samaria, Israel's political and religious center, that had left them relatively uncontaminated by Israel's apostasy and more responsive to the requirements of the true God.

Obviously the people of Judah were united in their approval of Hezekiah's reform (v. 12). They and their Israelite kin began to gather in Jerusalem by the second month. First they cleared away the vestiges of heathenism that had survived from the days of Ahaz (v. 14; cf. 2 Kings 16:10–16), casting the debris into the Kidron Valley (cf. 29:16). Then they offered the Passover sacrifice on the fourteenth day, that day prescribed by the Mosaic legislation, though it was the second month and not the first (Exod. 12:6).

There still were many priests and Levites ceremonially unprepared to participate in the Passover ritual so these, embarrassed by their state of religious impurity (cf. 29:34), consecrated themselves and brought their offerings. More priests and Levites than usual were required because the people, who ordinarily offered their own family Passover sacrifices (cf. Exod. 12:3), could not do so now because many of them were also ritually unclean (v. 17). The pilgrims from the distant parts of Israel were especially lacking in meeting the requirements of the Law for Passover participation (cf. Exod. 12:43–49), but Hezekiah permitted them to do so anyway in light of the peculiar and extenuating circumstances in which they found themselves. Besides, Moses himself had made allowance for such irregular cases, even allowing the celebration, as Hezekiah was doing, to fall in the second rather than the first month (cf. Num. 9:10–14).

In a remarkable prayer in which he reflected the superiority of the interior devotion of the heart to the exterior exhibition of mere ritual, Hezekiah pleaded that the Lord might pardon those sincere worshipers who may not have met specific stipulations of the Law but whose every desire was to please God (vv. 18–19). In solid affirmation of this principle, the Lord heard and granted his favor (v. 20).

For seven days the Feast of Unleavened Bread (that which was introduced by the Passover and was actually part of it; cf. Exod. 12:15–20) continued in a spirit of joy and praise. The Levites particularly were caught up in the full meaning of those days and discharged their responsibilities with unusual spiritual insight and enthusiasm (vv. 21–22). In fact, the stated week of observance seemed too short a time in which to celebrate so by popular consent the festivities went on for another full week (cf. 7:8–10).

With a spirit of generous cooperation the king and officials provided a total of 2,000 bulls and 17,000 sheep and goats for the extra days of sacrifice (v. 24). So great was the joy, the chronicler said, that one would have to hark back to the days of Solomon to find anything comparable (cf. 7:8–10). Finally the convocation came to an end and the priests uttered words of benediction (cf. Num. 39:43), words that reached to the Lord in heaven itself (v. 27; cf. 6:21, 30, 33, 39).

Thus revived, the Israelite pilgrims went out into the

countryside of Judah on their way home and destroyed the sacred stones (the *maṣṣēbôth;* cf. 14:3), Asherah poles, high places, and altars wherever they found them. They did the same throughout Benjamin, Ephraim, and Manasseh until at last they arrived in their own dwelling places (31:1).

3. Reorganization of Religious Personnel (31:2–21)

In line with the prescriptions of the Mosaic legislation, Hezekiah undertook the task of reorganizing and reestablishing the structures of public worship. This was necessary because of the neglect and deterioration that resulted from the apostate regime of Ahaz and it was inspired as well by the spirit of reformation engendered by the Great Passover.

His principal concern was to care for the priests and Levites whose public offerings and personal support had fallen off badly. He therefore divided them up into their appropriate divisions so that they could serve in all the capacities attendant to their respective offices and according to the schedule established by long precedent (v. 2; cf. 1 Chron. 24:1–31).

Next Hezekiah commanded that the people, following his own example, give the necessary offerings to sustain the daily sacrifices as well as those of the stated festival days. They were also to be mindful of the need to support the priests and Levites for this was their sole source of income, at least ideally (vv. 3–4; cf. Num. 18:8–32).

Gladly the people responded with their gifts of produce and livestock. From the scattered towns of Judah as well as Jerusalem they came with the tithes of all their labor, laying them in heaps before the temple. For four months they did so and when in the seventh month of the year Hezekiah saw all they had brought, he praised God and blessed his people for their generosity (vv. 5–8).

The king then asked the priests and Levites about this great accumulation of goods, presumably to ascertain if it was adequate for their needs. Azariah the chief priest assured Hezekiah that the bounty of the people was more than enough for the piles that he saw represented the surplus after the priests and Levites had taken what they needed (vv. 9–10). The Lord's blessing of which the priest spoke (v. 10) was the abundant harvests that began with the wheat crop in the third month (the Feast of Pentecost, v. 7; cf. Lev. 23:15–22) and ended with the ingathering of the orchards and vineyards in the seventh (the Feast of Tabernacles, v. 7; cf. Lev. 23:33–39).

To care for the superabundance Hezekiah authorized the construction or refurbishing of storerooms in the temple. Conaniah was appointed supervisor of these facilities and his brother Shimei and ten other men assisted him (vv. 11-13). Kore, the son of Imnah, the keeper of the East Gate, was responsible for the offerings brought to the Lord for the purpose of redistribution to the priests living in outlying towns (vv. 14–15). He had the help of six other Levites in this work of providing from freewill offerings the basic necessities of these servants of the Lord (cf. Exod. 29:26–28; Lev. 7:31–34).

Kore and his associates also tended to the needs of potential priests, boys three years old and older who were registered already in the priestly genealogies and who would someday fill that office. The system of support was thus according to genealogical records and also, in the case of Levites twenty years old and older, according to criteria such as particular responsibilities and divisions. Obviously the entire families of the ministers of the Lord were included for they, like their husbands and fathers, were also wholly committed to the Lord's work and wholly dependent on the community for their livelihood (vv. 16–18; cf. Num. 18:21–24).

Finally, priests who did not live in either Jerusalem or within the walls of a designated priestly community came in for their share (cf. Num. 35:2–5). There were certain persons responsible to see that these were not overlooked provided they were duly registered in the genealogies (v. 19).

By caring for the servants of the Lord in obedience to God's laws and ordinances, Hezekiah enjoyed success and prosperity (vv. 20–21). He fully recognized that the worship of the Lord could not be adequately undertaken until his human instruments enjoyed the sustenance that allowed them to provide the requisite leadership in it.

4. The Invasion of Sennacherib (32:1–23)

According to 2 Kings 18:13, Sennacherib king of Assyria invaded Judah and besieged Jerusalem in the fourteenth year of Hezekiah. As argued above, this was the year 701 B.C. (29:1). Ahaz, Hezekiah's father, had entered into an alliance with the Assyrian king Tiglath-Pileser as early as 732 B.C. (cf. 28:16–21) but Hezekiah broke the treaty after Ahaz died and Sargon (722–705) became king of Assyria (cf. 2 Kings 18:7). Since Sargon was occupied with pressing concerns in the Babylonian provinces of his empire, he was not able to force Hezekiah into submission. Once those problems were redressed, however, Sargon's successor Sennacherib decided to teach Hezekiah a lesson. Hence, the occasion for the chronicler's account here.

The first stage of Sennacherib's conquest involved the siege of Judah's fortified cities, no doubt the very ones that Solomon and his successors had built and rebuilt over the years (cf. 2 Chron. 8:6; 11:5–12; 14:6; 26:9–10; 27:4). While the Assyrians were thus occupied, Hezekiah took measures to protect Jerusalem against what he knew to be certain attack. First he had the springs and other water supplies blocked off from enemy use (vv. 3–4). Exactly how this was done is not clear but the author of Kings seems to link it with the construction of a tunnel that connected the city to the springs outside the walls. These springs and the tunnel must have been concealed to prevent the use of the water by the Assyrians and the interruption of its flow to the city (cf. 2 Kings 20:20; 2 Chron. 32:30).

Next Hezekiah and his fellow leaders ordered that the city walls be repaired and fortified with additional towers. Then they added a wall around the existing perimeter and reinforced the terraces (that is, the Millo; cf. 1 Kings 9:24) that supported the foundations of the walls. Finally his craftsmen manufactured a great quantity of offensive and defensive equipment (v. 5).

When all was ready Hezekiah organized his people militarily and assembled them at the plaza near the main gate of the city. He urged them not to be afraid for their God, he said, was greater than the human strength that fortified the Assyrians (vv. 6–8; cf. 2 Kings 6:16). Encouraged, the people waited to see what would come to pass.

Meanwhile Sennacherib had been attempting to force the city of Lachish into submission (v. 9; cf. 11:9 where Lachish is listed as one of Rehoboam's fortress cities). While occupied with this, he sent a delegation the 30 miles northeast to Jerusalem to demand that Hezekiah submit and surrender the capital. In a message designed to demoralize the people, Sennacherib asked why they thought they could survive his attack. The words of Hezekiah, he continued, were nothing but a vain and empty hope that would lead to nothing but starvation (vv. 10–11).

Sennacherib continued his communication by reminding the people of Jerusalem that their God would no longer be effective precisely because Hezekiah had removed his high places and altars and had limited him to only one sacred place (v. 12). This naive view of the Assyrian king was based, of course, on a failure to distinguish between the false gods whose shrines Hezekiah had destroyed and the one true God whose worship was limited to the temple. He imagined that the Lord would be offended by the lack of multiple shrines when, in fact, the centrality of worship was at the very heart of Israelite faith (cf. Deut. 12:5–7).

Continuing his taunt, Sennacherib boasted that the gods of all the other nations had been unable to protect their devotees from Assyrian destruction. This being the case, how would their one God be of any help to Judah? To rely on the false promises of Hezekiah would lead to nothing but ruin (vv. 13–15).

Again and again the Assyrians repeated their propaganda, charging that the God of Israel was impotent and unable to deliver (vv. 16–17). At last they resorted to the strategem of addressing the population directly by crying out to them in Hebrew. They alleged that the God of Jerusalem was like any other god—he was the product of human manufacture (v. 19)!

Terrified, Hezekiah enlisted the aid of Isaiah the prophet (cf. Isa. 37:1–7) and together they sought the face of the Lord in prayer (v. 20; cf. Isa. 37:14–35). In dramatic response the Lord sent an angel who wiped out the Assyrian army (v. 21; 2 Kings 19:35 states that the number of the slain was 185,000). At once Sennacherib lifted his siege of Lachish (presumably he personally was still there; cf. Isa. 36:2) and returned ignominiously to his own land. Though the chronicler does not suggest a passing of time (v. 21b), some twenty years after his ill-fated Jerusalem campaign (that is, in 681 B.C.) Sennacherib fell victim to assassination by his own sons while he was at worship in the temple of his god Nisroch in Nineveh (cf. Isa. 37:38).

Ironically, while Hezekiah's God had saved him, Sennacherib's could not save Sennacherib. The chronicler relates, in fact, that the Lord saved Hezekiah and his people from many similar emergencies, so much so that the peoples of many nations brought gifts of tribute to Hezekiah and his God (vv. 22–23; cf. 2 Kings 20:12).

5. Summary and Conclusion of Hezekiah's Reign (32:24–33)

Though the chronicler's account of the reign of Hezekiah is positive and favorable overall, he does mention an incident (greatly elaborated in 2 Kings 20:1–11 and Isa. 38:1–8) in which the godly king suffered what appeared to be a terminal illness. He prayed for a sign that he would be healed (cf. 2 Kings 20:11), a request that was granted along with the addition of fifteen more years of life (2 Kings 20:6). Because he failed to respond properly to God's gracious intervention, becoming instead filled with pride, the Lord became angry with him and his nation and would have punished them had Hezekiah not repented (vv. 24–26).

The reason for the pride may well be indicated by the list of accomplishments in vv. 27–30. He enjoyed riches and honor, he had accumulated and made provision to store all manner of valuables, such as silver, gold, precious stones, spices, and shields, and he had prepared facilities to accommodate the abundant harvests with which the Lord had blessed the land (vv. 27–28). He had also constructed villages surrounded by vast flocks and herds (v. 29). Not least was the design and construction of the water systems of Jerusalem that allowed the city to survive sieges. The chronicler suggests that this project involved the damming up of the waters of the Gihon spring in the Kidron Valley and rerouting them through tunnels to the west side of the city (v. 30).

Again there is a negative note for the narrator briefly alludes to the story of the envoys sent by Merodach-Baladan, the infamous Babylonian rebel against Assyria (cf. 2 Kings 20:12). They had come ostensibly to congratulate Hezekiah on his recovery from illness (that is, the fulfillment of the miraculous sign of 2 Kings 20:8–11; cf. 2 Chron. 32:31), but more likely to enlist his support against their Assyrian overlords. In any case, Hezekiah opened up his treasuries for the Babylonians to see, an act of pride that brought a scathing denunciation and prophecy of judgment from Isaiah (2 Kings 20:16–18; Isa. 39:5–7). All that the chronicler says is that the incident occurred so that God could test Hezekiah to know what was in his heart (v. 31). Obviously this was for Hezekiah's benefit so that he might understand the consequences of pride.

Characteristically, the historian closes the account of Hezekiah by citing other writings that add information, in this case both the works of Isaiah and the "book of the kings of Judah and Israel" (v. 32), probably the biblical Books of 1 and 2 Kings. As a godly king he was interred with his ancestors in the royal tombs of Jerusalem, honored and lamented by his people, and succeeded on the throne by his son Manasseh (v. 33).

E. The Reign of Manasseh (33:1–20)

Manasseh, the evil son of Hezekiah (v. 2), reigned for fifty-five years, the first eleven of which (697–686) were as co-regent with his father. His independent rule then was from 686 to 642.

His early years after Hezekiah's death were virtually a contradiction in every respect of what his father had stood for. He rebuilt the high places, reinstalled the Baal altars and Asherah poles, and devoted himself to the worship of astral deities (the "starry hosts"). These, of course, were the divinities thought to exist behind the stars, sun, moon, and planets—a notion particularly prominent in Mesopotamia (cf. Deut. 4:19; Ezek. 8:16). So taken up by this novelty was Manasseh that he erected altars to these gods of the heavens within the sacred courts of the temple itself (vv. 3–5), the place reserved exclusively for the Name (or presence) of the Lord (cf. 7:16).

Moreover, he emulated the heinous sin of his grandfather Ahaz (cf. 28:3) by offering his children as human sacrifices in the Valley of Ben Hinnom (v. 6). Like no king before he engaged in sorcery, divination, witchcraft, and the use of mediums and spiritists, all of which were roundly condemned in the Law (cf. Lev. 19:31; 20:6, 27; Deut. 18:9–12). The first three practices had to do with efforts to understand and manipulate the gods, while the other two were in the realm of necromancy, communication with the dead.

Most abominable of all perhaps was the desecration of the temple by an image Manasseh set up within its very chambers (v. 7). Its nature and identity are not further elaborated but again it occupied the place built for the habitation of the Lord alone. This was the climax of a series of defections from the Lord that led the people into apostasy worse than any in their past (v. 9) and that would lead to their judgment at the hand of the Lord (v. 8).

Heedless of the warnings that God graciously gave them, Manasseh and his people soon found themselves in the hands of Esar Haddon (or perhaps Ashurbanipal), king of Assyria, who led the king of Judah away like a wild bull with a ring in its nose (vv. 10–11). But then, in captivity, Manasseh repented of his sins against God, who heard his sincere prayer and brought him back to Jerusalem (vv. 12–13). Once and for all Manasseh came to understand that the Lord is God and there is no record of further covenant unfaithfulness (v. 13b).

Turning now to the positive side of Manasseh's reign, the chronicler relates facts concerning his construction projects, such as the rebuilding of the eastern wall of Jerusalem. It commenced west of the Gihon spring in the Kidron Valley (cf. 32:30) and ran north and then west to the Fish Gate, which was at the extreme northwest corner of the city (cf. Neh. 3:3). The project then followed the eastern wall south to the old city of Ophel and completely surrounded the hill on which it lay with a higher defense (v. 14).

Manasseh also remanned the fortified cities of Judah, likely to forestall more Assyrian incursions; dismantled the images and altars he had installed throughout Jerusalem; and reintroduced the worship of the true God by a service of consecration (vv. 15–16). The only caveat the chronicler shares is that the people continued to sacrifice at the high places. Even so, he says, they sacrificed to the Lord there and not to idols (v. 17; cf. 1:3).

In conclusion the historian points out that other documents

of Manasseh's reign such as his prayer (evidently that offered while in captivity; cf. vv. 12–13) and the messages of the prophets God had sent to him could be located in "the annals of the kings of Israel" (v. 18; cf. 1 Kings 14:14). Israel, of course, is a common designation in Chronicles for all the chosen nation without respect to the division between Israel and Judah (cf. 20:34; 21:2; 23:2). That same prayer and further information concerning Manasseh's apostasy prior to his repentance may be found, the chronicler says, in the records of Hozai (v. 19, NASB). This enigmatic source may better be understood as a corruption of the Hebrew word *ḥôzîm*, which means "seers."

Though he had repented and had been restored to Jerusalem, Manasseh was buried in his palace rather than in the royal tombs. His young son Amon next occupied the throne (v. 20).

F. The Reign of Amon (33:21–25)

Manasseh's son Amon apparently learned little or nothing from his father's experience of captivity and repentance for he practiced the same wicked idolatry as his father had, without ever returning to the Lord. In fact, the chronicler says, Amon's two short years (642–640 B.C.) were marked by a steady increase in guiltiness before God (vv. 21–23).

For unspecified reasons, Amon's own officials assassinated him. These conspirators in turn lost their lives to "the people of the land" who appointed Josiah king in his father Amon's place (vv. 24–25). The phrase "people of the land" refers to the masses or peasants rather than the aristocracy. On occasion they would rise up and assert their will in opposition to other political and/or socioeconomic elements (cf. 22:1; 23:21; 26:1; 36:1). Usually (as here no doubt) they were the conservatives who were eager to maintain Judean independence and to preserve the Mosaic traditions.

Since Josiah was clearly anti-Assyrian (cf. 2 Kings 23:29), many scholars believe that Amon was assassinated by anti-Assyrians who were interested in placing one of their own on Judah's throne. There seems little doubt that Amon and his father Manasseh before him were inclined to lend their support, if not their total allegiance, to Assyria.

G. The Reign of Josiah (34:1–35:27)

1. Josiah's Reformation (34:1–33)

Josiah was only eight years old when he began to reign so he must have been under the governorship of some party or other, probably representatives of "the people of the land" who had put him in power. He ruled for thirty-one years (640–609) but died even so a young man, a casualty of war against Egypt (35:24).

Since he was so young at his accession, Josiah pursued no policies on his own for several years. By his eighth year, however, he began to seek the will of God by instituting wide-ranging measures of reformation. These and other deeds provided a basis for the assessment of Josiah that he did what was right, walking unswervingly in the ways of David (vv. 2–3a).

The first concrete step in reformation was in Josiah's twelfth year when he was twenty. This consisted of the removal of high places, Asherah poles, and all kinds of idols from Jerusalem (v. 3). These objects he reduced to rubble, scattering their fragments over the graves of those who had used them in their heathen worship (v. 4). Moreover, he burned the bones of the apostate priests on their very altars, a visible act of repudiation of the religious corruption of his fathers which he extended beyond Jerusalem and Judah to Manasseh, Ephraim, Simeon, and even Naphtali (vv. 5–7).

This way of disposing of the priests is of special interest because of a story lacking in Chronicles but retained in 2 Kings 23:15–20. It pertains to the great altar at Bethel, the site of the illicit worship of the Lord established by Jeroboam, the first king of Israel (23:15; cf. 1 Kings 13:1). An unnamed prophet of Judah had predicted that the time would come when a son of David, Josiah by name, would sacrifice the wicked priests of Bethel upon that very altar and would burn their bones upon it (1 Kings 13:2). Now the time had come so Josiah slew the priests of the high places and burned their bones on the altar at Bethel (2 Kings 23:20). He then destroyed the altar and the high place of Bethel and others throughout the cities of Samaria (2 Kings 23:15, 19). In this remarkable way the Lord confirmed his word three hundred years later.

By Josiah's eighteenth year (622 B.C.), when he had reached the age of twenty-six, he had completed the work of eliminating the vestiges of paganism throughout the land. He then turned his attention to the temple, which was in a deplorable physical condition. He instructed Shaphan the secretary (v. 15), Maaseiah the mayor of Jerusalem, and Joah the recorder (or chronicler) to undertake its repairs. Money had already been collected by the Levites from throughout Israel and Judah and this they turned over to Hilkiah the high priest (vv. 8–9).

The funds were then distributed to the supervisors of the project who paid the various workmen for the materials they would use in the restoration of the temple, materials such as stone and timbers (vv. 10–11).

Jahath and Obadiah, Levites of the clan of Merari, and Zechariah and Meshullam, who were Kohathite Levites, were in charge overall. Under them were other Levites who, interestingly enough, are described as skillful musicians (v. 12). This suggests, perhaps, a spiritual and aesthetic sensitivity appropriate to the sacred work of temple reconstruction. These were foremen over the labor gangs that actually did the physical labor. Other Levites participated as secretaries, scribes, and doorkeepers in assignments whose purpose is not otherwise specified.

In the course of bringing the building funds out of the place in the temple prepared for their safekeeping, Hilkiah the priest happened upon the copy of the Book of the Law of Moses which had apparently been hidden there some time before (v. 14). Many modern scholars, on the basis of certain tradition-critical theories, assume that this was a scroll of Deuteronomy that was not Mosaic at all (except possibly in its oral nucleus) but the product of a long period of tradition culminated in a written form by a final editor or editors known as the "deuteronomist." There is no conclusive evidence that this is the case and no reason to deny that Hilkiah found a copy of the entire Law, the Torah (Genesis through Deuteronomy), written originally by Moses.

Hilkiah at once brought the scroll (or scrolls) to Shaphan the secretary who in turn notified the king of its existence. Shaphan reported on the progress of the work, concluding his report with

the finding of the scroll itself from which he proceeded to read
(vv. 15–18). He had hardly begun before Josiah was struck with
the import of its message. Tearing his robes in anguish and
contrition, he ordered Hilkiah, Shaphan, and other officials to
seek someone who could interpret the meaning of what the
scroll contained, particularly its relevance to the nation that had
so long lived in disobedience to its tenets and covenant
requirements (vv. 19–21).

It seems almost unbelievable in a day of mass publication
that there was a time when the entire written tradition of Israel
had perished except for one copy hidden and then "acciden-
tally" rediscovered in the temple. How this came about is not
altogether clear but it seems that the apostasy of the long reign
of Manasseh had been so thorough that it extended to the
purging of every last copy but one of the Law of Moses (cf.
33:1–9). Some pious priest no doubt had rescued one copy and
hid it prayerfully in a secret place in the temple. There it was
found by Hilkiah and made available to godly Josiah.

Hilkiah and his colleagues went straight to the "Second
District," a suburb of Jerusalem (cf. Zeph. 1:10), where they
found Huldah the prophetess. She was the wife of Shallum who
was keeper of the wardrobes, a reference to the place of either
the royal or priestly garments. At once she began to share the
revelation of the Lord concerning the scroll. He was about to
bring upon the land and its people all the curses written in the
scroll (cf. Lev. 26:14–30; Deut. 28:15–68) because of their
idolatry (vv. 22–25). Josiah himself would be spared, however,
because he had responded humbly and repentantly when he
had heard the message it contained. He would not have to
witness the awful calamity that would befall his nation (that is,
the Babylonian destruction and Exile; cf. 36:17–21) but would
die and be buried in peace (vv. 26–28; cf. 35:24) before that
happened.

When he heard the report, Josiah gathered a great assembly
before the temple, a throng composed of a cross section of all the
nation from the highest to the lowest levels of society. He then
began to read the Book of the Covenant (v. 30), a term referring
most likely to either the section by that name in Exodus (chs.
20–23) or the Book of Deuteronomy. When he finished he

renewed his covenant vows as king (cf. Deut. 17:18–20) and then led the people to do the same, according to all the mandates of the ancient covenant texts (vv. 31–32).

As attestation to the genuineness of the commitment, Josiah eradicated the remnants of idolatry from the land. The rest of his days he lived in obedience to that commitment as did his fellow citizens. As long as he lived Judah faithfully followed the Lord (v. 33).

2. The Great Passover (35:1–19)

In the eighteenth year of Josiah, the same year as that of the discovery of the Law scroll in the temple (v. 19), Josiah celebrated a great Passover in Jerusalem (v. 1). Since that occasion presupposes a suitable setting and climate, the reformation must have preceded the Passover. The Passover fell on the fourteenth day of the first month but that is in terms of the religious calendar. The civil calendar dated the first month six months earlier, in September/October, so the reformation took place between then and March/April, the month of Passover. Both could, therefore, have occurred in Josiah's eighteenth year.

The king himself issued instructions about the service. He counseled the Levites first to place the ark in the temple where it belonged, a command that seems to suggest that the ark had been removed, perhaps during the refurbishing. Next Josiah divided the Levites up by their traditional divisions (v. 4) and arranged them in and about the temple according to their respective responsibilities (v. 5). Then he instructed them to consecrate themselves and to prepare for the slaughter of the Passover lamb on behalf of the general population (v. 6).

Out of his personal largess Josiah provided 30,000 sheep and goats and 3,000 cattle (v. 7; cf. the totals for Hezekiah's Passover in 30:24). In addition his officials gave generously. Hilkiah the priest and his two fellow temple administrators donated 2,600 Passover offerings (that is, sheep and goats) and 300 cattle. The leaders of the Levites also were not slack, presenting among the six of them 5,000 sheep and goats and 500 head of cattle. The grand total of 37,600 sheep and goats and 3,800 cattle was an immense tribute to the generosity of Judah's leaders.

When all was ready the officiants offered the Passover lambs. The priests sprinkled the blood as prescribed (Exod. 12:21–22) and the Levites skinned them and the other animals in preparation for their burning on the altar and division among the people (vv. 11–13; cf. Exod. 12:4, 8–9). The same was done with the cattle. Only the lambs and goats were suitable for Passover and daily burnt offerings (Exod. 12:3; 29:38–45) so the cattle were for fellowship or peace offerings (cf. Lev. 3:1–5).

After they had attended to the needs of the people, the Levites made offerings for themselves and the priests since the priests were so busy with their work that they had no time to care for their personal sacrifices (v. 14). The Levites who were not engaged in the sacrificing *per se* did not need to leave their duties as musicians or gatekeepers because the other Levites were considerate of them and provided them with their share of the fellowship offerings (v. 15).

At last the Passover festival was over and the seven-day Feast of Unleavened Bread along with it (cf. 30:13–22). Not since Samuel, notes the chronicler, had such a Passover been held, including that of Hezekiah (vv. 16–18).

3. The Death of Josiah (35:20–27)

In 609 B.C., thirteen years after the great Passover of Josiah, Neco king of Egypt (609–594 B.C.) moved north through Palestine to launch an attack against the Babylonians who were on their way to Haran and Carchemish to do battle with the Assyrians. The Assyrians had declined abruptly from the pinnacle of power they had enjoyed just a generation before. They had lost virtually everything to the Babylonians (or Chaldeans) by 612 B.C. and now entrenched themselves at their two strongholds on the Upper Euphrates.

Egypt was more afraid of the rising Babylonians than the falling Assyrians and so Neco tried to stave off Assyria's defeat by intercepting the Babylonians. Josiah, an ally of the Babylonians (probably because of the Merodach–Baladan visit; cf. 32:31), decided to interfere by preventing the northward march of the Egyptian army (v. 20). This would prove to be a fatal mistake.

In a most remarkable statement the historian says that Neco

sent messengers to Josiah to warn him not to get involved in this matter for God had told the Egyptian that he was with him and not with Josiah (v. 21). That this was not a mere ploy is clear from the following comment: "He [Josiah] would not listen to what Neco had said at God's command" (v. 22). God thus chose to reveal himself through a heathen unbeliever, a strange but not unprecedented thing (cf. Gen. 20:3; 41:25; Num. 22:9; Dan. 2:28).

As a result of his failure to discern the will of God mediated through the proud Egyptian, Josiah was severely wounded on the battlefield of Megiddo. Hoping to escape with his life, he fled to Jerusalem in a chariot where he shortly died (vv. 23–24). With great lament his subjects buried him in the royal sepulchres of Jerusalem. So celebrated and popular was Josiah that Jeremiah the prophet composed laments that the singers of Israel were still singing down to the time of the chronicler himself (v. 25a). Though there may be some evidence of these compositions in the canonical books of Jeremiah (cf. Jer. 22:10; Lam. 4:20), most likely the "laments" (v. 25b) refers to a writing no longer extant.

As for other events of Josiah's glorious reign, the chronicler says they are documented in the "book of the kings of Israel and Judah," perhaps the biblical Books of Kings.

H. The Reign of Jehoahaz (36:1–4)

The death of Josiah, sudden and unexpected as it was, had the potential of unleashing all kinds of division and instability in the kingdom for he had four sons, all of whom could contend for the throne (cf. 1 Chron. 3:15). The eldest, Johanan, never appears in the narratives but the other three—Jehoiakim, Zedekiah, and Jehoahaz (otherwise Shallum; Jer. 22:11)—all became kings of Judah. For reasons not apparent in the accounts, Jehoahaz, the next to youngest, advanced ahead of the other two for the "people of the land" set him on his father's throne (v. 1).

Unfortunately, the defeat of Egypt by Nebuchadnezzar and the Babylonians at Haran in 609 did not result in an Egyptian withdrawal to their homeland but only to the region south of the Euphrates. Palestine therefore remained under Egyptian control and Judah for a time was an Egyptian vassal state. This explains why Neco king of Egypt replaced Jehoahaz after only three months (in 609) with his brother Eliakim whom he renamed Jehoiakim (v. 4). Neco then took Jehoahaz prisoner to Egypt and extracted from the Judean coffers a tribute of 100 talents (3 3/4 tons) of silver and a talent (75 pounds) of gold (v. 3).

I. The Reign of Jehoiakim (36:5-8)

Jehoiakim, the second eldest son of Josiah, reigned for eleven years (609-598 B.C.), a rule that was evil and disastrous for Judah. After the Battle of Carchemish in 605, Nebuchadnezzar of Babylon had driven Egypt out of Palestine and had brought Jehoiakim (and Judah) under his control (cf. 2 Kings 24:7). Shortly thereafter (in 602) Jehoiakim rebelled against Babylon (cf. 2 Kings 24:1) so Nebuchadnezzar returned to Jerusalem to put down the insurrection and to take Jehoiakim back with him to Babylon (v. 6). Evidently, Nebuchadnezzar changed his mind about deporting Jehoiakim for the records apart from Chronicles are unanimous in describing his place of death and burial as Jerusalem (cf. 2 Kings 24:6; Jer. 22:18-19).

The Babylonians did carry off some of the sacred furnishings of the temple and placed them in their own pagan temples in Babylon (v. 7). These judgments fell upon the nation because of the wicked acts of Jehoiakim, further elaboration of which, the chronicler notes, appears in the "book of the kings of Israel and Judah" (v. 8; cf. 35:27).

J. The Reign of Jehoiachin (36:9-10)

Jehoiachin was a son of Jehoiakim who reigned for only three months (about 598/597). Just prior to Jehoiakim's death he had rebelled against the Babylonians once again (implied in 2 Kings 24:10) thus requiring another campaign by Nebuchadnezzar to the West. Before the Babylonians could reach Jerusalem Jehoiakim died leaving his young son (the chronicler says he was eight years old but cf. the better reading 18 in 2 Kings 24:8) to bear the brunt of retaliation.

For his evil deeds and those of his nation, Jehoiachin went into Babylonian Exile along with treasures of the temple that had escaped earlier looting (v. 10). The chronicler is silent on the matter but 2 Kings 25:27–30 relates that Jehoiachin lived on in Babylon until at least the thirty-seventh year of his captivity (560 B.C.) and that he was then put on a royal pension by Evil-Merodach King of Babylon for the rest of his life.

K. The Reign of Zedekiah and the Fall of Jerusalem (36:11–21)

The last king of Judah was also a son of Josiah. His description as "brother" of Jehoiachin (v. 10) reflects the Hebrew way of indicating a close relative (cf. 2 Kings 24:17–18). His reign of eleven years (597–586 B.C.) was evil (v. 12) despite the constant warnings of Jeremiah the prophet (cf. Jer. 21:3–7; 32:5). His hardness of heart was emulated by all the religious and political leadership of Judah who insisted on mimicking the idolatrous practices of their pagan neighbors, thus desecrating God's holy temple (v. 14).

Zedekiah, moreover, compounded his sin of rebelling against the Lord by breaking his faith with Nebuchadnezzar (v. 13). This resulted in yet another western campaign by the Babylonians, which commenced in 588 and ended with the violent overthrow of Jerusalem in 586 (cf. 2 Kings 25:1–4). The chronicler recounts that Nebuchadnezzar, as an instrument of God's judgment upon his disobedient and unrepentant people (vv. 15–16), slew the citizens of Jerusalem mercilessly, carried off the treasures of both temple and palace, and utterly demolished the physical structures of the city including the temple and the palace (vv. 17–19).

Notable by its omission in the present record is any reference to the fate of Zedekiah, but 2 Kings 25:1–7 reports that he tried to escape the city but was captured by the Babylonians, taken to the military outpost of Riblah in Syria, blinded, and carried off to Babylon. His whereabouts after that remains a mystery.

The chronicler does relate that the survivors of the massacre at Jerusalem were spirited off to Babylon where they, and other Judeans who had preceded them, remained until the liberating decree of Cyrus, which came with the fall of Babylon to Persia in 539 B.C. (v. 20). The time in exile was seventy years (v. 21), probably to be dated from the first deportation of 605 B.C. to the laying of the foundations of the post-exilic temple in 536 B.C. (cf. Ezra 3:8). This length of time was prophesied by Jeremiah (25:12; cf. 29:10; Dan. 9:2; Zech. 7:5) but the chronicler gives the reason for the number seventy. The Law of Moses required that the land lie fallow every seventh year (Lev. 25:4). Failure to do this would bring about the Lord's judgment in which the land would lie fallow by virtue of the people's absence from it (Lev. 26:33–35). For seventy sevens of years (or 490) this attention to the Law had been neglected. Now the seventy years of exile would compensate. Since four-hundred-and-ninety years prior to 538 (the decree of Cyrus) would yield a date of 1028 B.C., prior even to David's reign, it is likely that the numbers are not to be pressed too literally though that is not out of the question.

L. The Decree of Cyrus (36:22–23)

Babylon fell to the Persian armies under Cyrus in 539 B.C. and within a few months this enlightened leader issued a decree permitting all Babylonian captives, including the Jews, to return to their homelands. In his own inscription Cyrus attributed his beneficent policy to the Babylonian god Marduk but the biblical writers correctly understood that it was the Lord God of Israel who inspired him to do so (v. 22; cf. Ezra 1:1–4). The Persian king was but an instrument of the Lord prophesied by Jeremiah (cf. Jer. 25:12) to be the means of effecting his people's deliverance and restoration (v. 23; cf. 35:22 where God spoke through another heathen king).

The message of the Lord through Cyrus was that he would authorize the Persian to be instrumental in the rebuilding of the temple of Solomon that Nebuchadnezzar had leveled to the ground (v. 23; cf. Isa. 44:28–45:7). Cyrus also permitted the Jewish exiles to return to their homes in Jerusalem and Judah so that they might continue the redemptive covenant purpose for which God had called them in the first place.

Thus the chronicler completed his work with an eye to the future. He had fulfilled his purpose of locating Israel under a messianic kingship within the context of universal history. The course of Israel's history within that context had not always been one of obedient covenant fulfillment; indeed, it climaxed in destruction and deportation. But there was a day yet to come, a day in which the sure promises to David would find perfect realization in the Son of David, Jesus Christ the Lord.

For Further Study

1. The historical background of the Assyrian conquest of Samaria in 732 B.C. and that of Samaria in 721 B.C. is complicated but essential to the understanding of Israel's fall and Judah's peril. Read a history of Israel for this period in order to place events in proper sequence.

2. What was the role of Isaiah the prophet, especially in the court of Hezekiah? Is it appropriate for a Christian clergyman to be involved in political activity as Isaiah was? What are the similarities and differences between ancient Israel's sociopolitical life and that of modern states? How do these affect the matter of church and state?

3. Outline the steps followed by Josiah in bringing about religious reformation in his time. Can these steps be followed today in the church and can one expect the same results?

Bibliography

Ackroyd, Peter R. *I and II Chronicles, Ezra, Nehemiah.* Torch Bible Commentaries. London: SCM Press, 1973.

Braun, Roddy. *1 Chronicles* in *Word Biblical Commentary,* Vol. 14. Waco: Word, 1986.

Coggins, R. J. *The First and Second Book of the Chronicles.* New York: Cambridge, 1976.

Curtis, Edward L. and A. A. Madsen. *A Critical and Exegetical Commentary on The Book of Chronicles.* Edinburgh: T. T. Clark, 1910.

Ellison, H. L., "1 and 2 Chronicles," *The New Bible Commentary: Revised.* Edited by D. Guthrie and J. A. Motyer. Grand Rapids: Eerdmans, 1970, pp. 369–394.

Elmslie, W. A. L. "The First and Second Books of Chronicles," in *The Interpreter's Bible,* Vol. 3. Edited by G. Buttrick *et al.* Nashville: Abingdon, 1954, pp. 341–548.

Herbert, A. S. "I and II Chronicles" in *Peake's Commentary on the Bible.* Edited by M. Black and H. H. Rowley. London: Thomas Nelson, 1962, pp. 357–369.

Keil, C. F. *The Books of Chronicles in Biblical Commentary on the Old Testament.* Grand Rapids: Eerdmans, n.d.

Myers, Jacob M. *I Chronicles* in *The Anchor Bible,* Vol. 12. Garden City, NY: Doubleday, 1965.

———. *II Chronicles* in *The Anchor Bible,* Vol. 13. Garden City, NY: Doubleday, 1965.

Sailhamer, John. *First and Second Chronicles.* Chicago: Moody, 1983.

Slotki, I. W. *Chronicles: Hebrew Text and English Translation with an Introduction and Commentary.* London: Soncino, 1952.

Williamson, H. G. M. *1 and 2 Chronicles* in *The New Century Bible Commentary.* Grand Rapids: Eerdmans, 1982.